Edmund Burke and the
Perennial Battle, 1789-1797

"This delightful book, learnedly introduced and annotated, distills to their essence Burke's reflections on a decisive decade. It is an invaluable resource for Burke scholars and Burkean citizens alike."

–**Gregory S. Weiner**, Assumption University

"This new collection condenses the best of Burke's late thought, making his timeless insights accessible to the general reader. A vital addition to any good library."

–**Marc Sidwell**, New Culture Forum

"Edmund Burke's writings of the era of the French Revolution provide ammunition for almost every variety of conservatism – liberal, reformist, or reactionary. Here is the armory."

–**Jerry Z. Muller**, Catholic University of America

"This volume is a vital resource for readers interested in the contribution to political thought of the great statesman Edmund Burke. Klein and Pino's anthology of writings offers a rich storehouse of insight and reflection arising out of Burke's engagement with the events of the French Revolution, illustrating some of his core values, and posing the question of how they might be relevant today."

–**Richard Bourke**, King's College, University of Cambridge, Author of *Empire & Revolution: The Political Life of Edmund Burke*

"This is a wonderful volume of Burke's most mature and most compelling thought, carefully curated and organized so as to be of maximal use to scholars and students of liberal thought. The introduction places Burke's thought and its seeming contradictions into the context of his times. The selections themselves place Burke's thought into the context of the life of a statesman aware of the delicate balance between principles and politics and of the tradeoffs involved in human life."

–**Lauren Hall**, Political Science, Rochester Institute of Technology

"What is Burke's political thought distilled to its essence? Daniel Klein and Dominic Pino capture it in this volume by selecting and annotating his prime quotations on the French Revolution from 1789 to 1797 with impressive discretion of judgment. And for those who think Burke's thoughts on the Revolution hold no pressing application to contemporary public affairs–and particularly for those who conflate empty change with judicious reform–Klein and Pino's deliciously provocative and eloquently written introduction, distilled to its essence, offers this sharp rejoinder: Guess again."

–**Gregory M. Collins**, Yale University, author of *Commerce and Manners in Edmund Burke's Political Economy*

"Dan Klein and Dominic Pino have brought the wisdom of Edmund Burke alive again in this judicious and comprehensive selection of his 'living voice' during the last momentous decade of his life. The crisp, cogent passages chosen by the editors highlight a thought at once conservative and liberal, committed to reform but never to radical innovation, and alert as no one before or after to the totalitarianism implicit in the Jacobin project to transform the world. Burke's famous self-description, that he loved 'a manly, moral, regulated liberty,' is evident on every page of this inspired compilation. And in an astute 'Introduction,' Klein and Pino show the coherence of Burke's noble project to combine 'liberty in policy' and 'stability in polity,' an endeavor as welcome today as it was in the closing decade of the eighteenth century."

–**Daniel J. Mahoney**, author of *The Statesman as Thinker: Portraits of Courage, Greatness, and Moderation (Encounter Books, 2022)*

"Among the challenges of teaching Burke are his zesty style and the dispersion of ideas across numerous texts written amidst shifting circumstances. Klein and Pino have done a great service in collecting key passages 1789 to 1797. Astutely selected and deftly annotated, the passages platform the voice, the personality, of Burke, with all its prophetic wisdom."

–**Richard Boyd**, Georgetown University

Edmund Burke and the Perennial Battle, 1789-1797

Edited with an introduction by
Daniel B. Klein and Dominic Pino

 **CL Press**

Published by CL PRESS
A project of the Fraser Institute
1770 Burrard Street, 4th Floor
Vancouver, BC V6J 3G7 Canada
www.clpress.net

Edmund Burke and the Perennial Battle, 1789-1797
Edited and with an introduction by
Daniel B. Klein and Dominic Pino

© 2022 by CL Press

First printed April 2022; corrected July 2022.

Published in partnership with
The Acton Institute
The Fund for American Studies
National Review Institute
and the Russell Kirk Center

Cover image: Edmund Burke (1729-1797), portrait by studio of
Sir Joshua Reynolds, oil on canvas, c.1769 or after.
IanDagnall Computing / Alamy Stock Photo

ISBN: 978-1-957698-00-7

Interior and cover design by Joanna Andreasson

Published by:

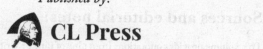 CL Press

A Project of:

In partnership with:

The
FUND for
AMERICAN
STUDIES

THE EDMUND BURKE SOCIETY
A Project of the Russell Kirk Center

NATIONAL REVIEW
INSTITUTE

Sources and editorial notes:

This volume provides quotations from nine of Burke's writings. The nine writings are shown in the Table of Contents. Each quotation is accompanied by a page citation to the Liberty Fund volume that contains the writing:

- The first, third, fourth, fifth, seventh, and eighth writings are contained in: Edmund Burke, *Further Reflections on the French Revolution*, ed. Daniel E. Ritchie, published by Liberty Fund, 1992.

- The sixth writing—which is not about revolutionary France but contains several worthy passages—is contained in Vol. 4 of *Selected Works of Edmund Burke: Miscellaneous Writings*, compiled and with a Foreword and Select Bibliography by Francis Canavan, published by Liberty Fund, 1999.

- *Reflections* is contained in: Edmund Burke, Reflections on the Revolution in France (1790), Vol. 2 of *Selected Works of Edmund Burke*, a new imprint of the Payne Edition. Foreword by Francis Canavan, published by Liberty Fund, 1999.

- *Letters on a Regicide Peace* is contained in: Edmund Burke, Letters on a Regicide Peace (1795). In Vol. 3 of *Selected Works of Edmund Burke*, a new imprint of the Payne Edition. Foreword and Biographical Note by Francis Canavan, published by Liberty Fund, 1999.

All italicization is original to Burke. We have very occasionally altered spelling or punctuation from the Liberty Fund text in minor ways, without notice, for example changing "it's" when meaning what we now mean by "its." In brackets [like these] we insert notes to clarify or explain bits of text.

Contents

Introduction

When we read texts from a bygone era that relate to the present, we often think things like, "It seems like the author was reading the news today," or, "How did the author know this was coming?" We marvel at the author's foresight, and we are surprised a text so old could be so relevant.

Marveling at the foresight of a long departed mind reflects a disbelief in that thing which people allege from time to time called human nature. The implicit belief undergirding the marveling is that some old, dead authors couldn't possibly have anything relevant to say to us today. They didn't even have smartphones! How could they know anything useful? It's certainly true that scientific progress has rendered many old beliefs to be wrong, and reading a physics textbook from 1825 will probably lead you astray. But any good insight in the humanities will be relevant for all time, whether the author intended it or not. If you take the word "humanities" seriously, you will see that the fields comprising it (art, literature, politics, philosophy, etc.) are about humans. Science, culture, and living standards have all changed a lot more than humans have over the course of recorded history. Biological evolution is a notoriously slow process, and if you're reading something that someone wrote down, no matter when it was written, the author and the humans he wrote about are close enough to us to be pretty much identical biologically.

Ancient religions produced many ideas, one, most clearly and famously put in the Book of Genesis, being the idea that we were all created in the image of God. Those who taught that didn't do any randomized controlled trials to come to that conclusion – they might say that God told them that. But no matter how they came to that conclusion, the idea is sublime, and it was full of implications. One natural implication of everyone being created in the image of God is that in some fundamental sense we are all the same. Modern science has confirmed that in some fundamental sense, we are. We are composed of cells organized in roughly the same way with predictable genetic structures and predictable responses to stimuli. Acetaminophen does the same thing in the body of a 60-year-old, South American woman as it does in the body of a 20-year-old, European man.

We had this insight long before we knew about the nervous system: A hot stove doesn't care whether you are rich or poor – it's going to burn your hand if you touch it. Hot stoves in 1800 burned people the same way hot stoves burn people today. People react in much the same way, and their skin burns in the same way. The common denominator is human. Humans haven't changed much in the past 10,000 years even though we live with technology and culture that would be utterly alien to an ancient Sumerian.

If an insight into human nature is good and accurate, it is timeless.

We should think of good and accurate insights in political philosophy in much the same way that we think of the insight that we shouldn't touch hot stoves. Politics is part of the humanities—or moral philosophy, as Adam Smith would have put it—and no matter how much technology we use, humans are a necessary participant in the political process. There is no politics on Jupiter. But so long as there have been humans on Earth, there have been struggles for power, organizations and hierarchies, violence hidden and overt, and efforts to make sense of it all—rhetoric and persuasion. We shouldn't be the least bit surprised when an author from the 1790s seems to be speaking directly to us in the present. If he were any good, we should actually expect it. The present compendium flows from our conviction that Edmund Burke was darned good.

***

Edmund Burke was a great political writer, so he seems to be speaking to us in the present. Irish-born yet devotedly British, Burke was a member of Parliament and a prolific writer on many issues in Britain in his time. Often seen as a father of conservatism, Burke's thought is much more complicated than merely opposing change. This book seeks to highlight the last part of Burke's career, with his most famous work, *Reflections on the Revolution in France*, as the chief starting point (though we include a few passages from a letter of November 1789). From the *Reflections* in 1790 and continuing until his death in 1797, Burke's publications focused on the new set of slogans, opinions, sentiments, manners, visions–modes of feeling, thinking, speaking, and acting–that he saw rising throughout Europe. Since 1789 that set of modes has been referred to as Jacobinism, radicalism, rationalism, dogmatism, and so on. No single word is adequate, but we will speak of it as radicalism. In the quotations provided here, Burke describes many aspects of the quasi-religion that was spreading like fire.

In his final years, Burke himself writes with burning vitality. But Burke's writings, speeches, and letters during the 40 years prior to 1790 offer much, much more, and they enrich our understanding of the material represented here. The present collection hopes to distill a special and timeless portion of his writings, but only a portion. If the student of Burke's thought wishes to find his important statements along the lines of the themes captured in this book prior to 1789, he or she should look especially at a draft speech that Burke wrote in 1782, but did not deliver, "Speech on the Reform of the Representation of the Commons in Parliament" (in *Miscella-*

neous Writings, Liberty Fund, 1999).

When you read the selections in this book, you will notice parallels to radicalism today. Many today would trace radicalism to thinkers like Karl Marx and ideologies like socialism and progressivism. But Burke was writing before Marx was born and before state-socialist visions were conceived, although there had appeared such works as Thomas More's *Utopia,* which probably was satirical, and Étienne-Gabriel Morelly's 1755 *Code of Nature,* which was obscure and also perhaps satirical—as well as Plato's *Republic.* Without a pinch of satire, Jean-Jacques Rousseau persistently aroused radical and socialist penchants, but he scarcely put forth a coherent vision of a socialist or fascist polity.

Radical philosophers and ideologies don't cause the natural human penchants and instincts that attract people to radicalism. Radical philosophies and ideologies are downstream of those penchants and instincts. In the works quoted in this book, Burke explores the threat, upstream and downstream, showing us the perennial battle we cannot help but involve ourselves in.

Breaking down political thought on the basis of support or opposition to change is woefully insufficient. Burke was a staunch defender of the British society in which he lived, but his most famous political positions often advocated altering the status quo. Burke's political activity may seem to contradict his philosophy, but the contradiction is only apparent. First, Burke makes a distinction between change and reformation that sheds light on how to view his political activities. Second, he was a liberal on some vital aspects of politics.

Burke retired from Parliament in 1794 and, never having been extraordinarily wealthy, was in danger of losing his home. In late 1794, Prime Minister William Pitt the Younger decided to award Burke a pension of 1,200 pounds per year. By 1795, Pitt also award-ed Burke two annuities directly from the crown, so Burke's annual pension totaled 3,700 pounds. (Pitt was chancellor of the exchequer as well as prime minister.) Members of Parliament were upset about Burke's pension for two reasons: They were excluded from Pitt's decision to grant the pension, and Burke had given a speech in 1780 that assailed pensions without parliamentary oversight.[1]

Burke responded to those attacks in 1796 with "A Letter to a Noble Lord." Burke's response to an apparent contradiction in his own day contains a resolution to the apparent contradiction in Burke's political thought. Burke outlines what he calls "a marked distinction between Change and Reformation."[2] He writes:

> [Change] alters the substance of the objects themselves; and gets rid of all their essential good, as well as of all the accidental evil annexed to them. Change is novelty; and whether it is to operate any one of the effects of reformation at all, or whether it may not contradict the very principle upon which reformation is desired, cannot be certainly known beforehand. Reform is, not a change in the substance, or in the primary modification of the object, but a direct application of a remedy to the grievance complained of. So far as that is removed, all is sure. It stops there; and if it fails, the substance which underwent the operation, at the very worst, is but where it was.[3]

Burke is opposed to changes but in favor of some reforms. The difference is best illustrated, fittingly, by the French Revolution. A

---

1. Daniel Ritchie, ed., *Further Reflections on the Revolution in France*, Indianapolis: Liberty Fund, 1992, pp. 277-278.

2. Ibid., p. 290.

3. Ibid.

few sentences later, Burke writes, "The French revolutionists complained of everything; they refused to reform any thing; and they left nothing, no nothing at all *unchanged*."[4] One of his problems with the revolutionists was their enthusiasm for change and disdain for reform. "To innovate is not to reform,"[5] Burke wrote.

Making the distinction between change and reform, however, raises the question of when reform is appropriate. If Burke were merely in favor of reform in general, it would be difficult to call him a conservative. Surely he earned the conservative label from something, and he did set up a presumption that must be overcome to merit reform in his "Speech on Fox's East India Bill." British policy in India was one of the political issues of his day about which Burke was most outspoken. The British East India Company had come to abuse the public's trust in it, and Burke's actions to rectify that situation demonstrate his ideal for reform instead of change.

In his speech, Burke outlines his belief that there are indeed reasons to alter the status quo. Chief among them are violations of natural rights. "The rights of men, that is to say, the natural rights of mankind, are indeed sacred things; and if any public measure is proved mischievously to affect them, the objection ought to be fatal to that measure, even if no charter at all could be set up against it."[6] He then contrasts the charter of the British East India Company with the Great Charter. He writes:

> *Magna charta* is a charter to restrain power, and to
> destroy monopoly. The East India Company charter is
> a charter to establish monopoly, and to create power.
> Political power and commercial monopoly are *not* the

---

4. Ibid., pp. 290-291. Italics in original.

5. Ibid., p. 290.

6. Francis Canavan, ed., *Miscellaneous Writings*, Indianapolis: Liberty Fund, 1999, p. 99.

rights of men; and the rights to them derived from char-
ters, it is fallacious and sophistical to call 'the chartered
rights of men'.[7]

Even so, the mere existence of an abuse of natural rights is not
enough for Burke to act for reform. He writes, "I feel an insuperable
reluctance in giving my hand to destroy any established institution
of government, upon a theory, however plausible it may be."[8] He
assuages that reluctance by setting up a series of four hurdles that
an abuse must clear in order to be worthy of reform.

First, "The object affected by the abuse should be great and
important."[9] He sees degrees in the importance of objects of public policy—he is not a monist by any stretch of the imagination. His
anti-monism extends also to the nature of the abuse; his second
criterion: "The abuse affecting this great object ought to be a great
abuse."[10] Even if the abuse is of an important object, not all abuses
are abusive enough to merit reform. Third, "It ought to be habitual, and not accidental."[11] Motives matter to Burke, and the mere
existence of a great abuse of a great object is not enough for reform.
Fourth and finally, "It ought to be utterly incurable in the body as
it now stands constituted."[12] Before even thinking about reforming
the institutions, look for remedy within the existing institutions.

Burke sees the importance of persuasion in reformation. The
hurdles are not strictly defined—what counts as great or important?
how often must an abuse occur to be habitual? etc.—so persuasion

---

7. Ibid., p. 100. Italics in original.

8. Ibid., p. 104.

9. Ibid., p. 105.

10. Ibid.

11. Ibid.

12. Ibid.

is going to be necessary to apply Burke's four-part test. After laying out the four parts, he writes, "All this ought to be made as visible to me as the light of the sun, before I should strike off an atom of [the East India Company's] charter."[13] He then proceeds to argue that the East India Company's abuses clear all four hurdles and the charter deserves reform. He does not argue that the substance of the object should be changed; he does not argue for decolonization. He argues that the terms of the East India Company's charter have not been kept, that grievance was complained of, and it is worthy of being corrected with Fox's bill.

Burke's desire for reform also arises from what he perceives to be the objects of his loyalty. He certainly sees himself as a loyal British subject, and there is no question he is proud of Great Britain. That being said, he sees his primary loyalty as one to the human race. In his speech on Fox's bill, Burke says he can't retain his faith in the East India Company because doing so would require him to "break the faith, the covenant, the solemn, original, indispensable oath, in which I am bound, by the eternal frame and constitution of things, to the whole human race."[14] Burke elaborates most fully on that allegiance in a different speech, "Speech to the Electors of Bristol."

He gave the speech at Bristol after winning his first election to Parliament in 1774. This speech contains some of the most famous words written on the legislator's job: "Your Representative owes you, not his industry only, but his judgment; and he betrays, instead of serving you, if he sacrifices it to your opinion."[15] Burke is wary of his constituents' opinions because he does not see himself as primarily obligated to them, but instead to the whole country:

---

13. Ibid.

14. Ibid., p. 155.

15. Ibid., p. 11.

Parliament is not a *Congress* of Ambassadors from different and hostile interests; which interests each must maintain, as an Agent and Advocate, against other Agents and Advocates; but Parliament is a *deliberative* Assembly of *one* Nation, with *one* Interest, that of the whole; where, not local Purposes, not local Prejudices ought to guide, but the general Good, resulting from the general Reason of the whole.[16]

Upon his election, Burke "is not a Member of Bristol, but he is a Member of *Parliament*."[17] His sense of a higher obligation necessitates some reforms on the lower plane of humanity.

For that reason Burke had no problem expressing his sympathy for Indians harmed by the East India Company—or for Africans under the yoke of slavery. In "Sketch of the Negro Code," Burke outlines his proposal to reform slavery with the goal of eventual abolition: "Rather than suffer it to continue as it is, I heartily wish it at an end."[18] He does not see political circumstances as allowing for rapid abolition, so he writes, "Taking for my basis that I had an incurable evil to deal with, I cast about how I should make it as small an evil as possible, and draw out of it some collateral good."[19]

Burke believed "nothing can be more uncertain than the operation of general principles, if they are not embodied in specifick regulations."[20] His sketch gives those regulations. He is clear-eyed about the evil he is confronting. The preamble to his sketch explains his motivation:

16. Ibid., p. 11-12. Italics in original.

17. Ibid., p. 12. Italics in original.

18. Ibid., p. 255.

19. Ibid., p. 256.

20. Ibid., p. 257.

> Whereas it is expedient, and conformable to the prin-
> ciples of true religion and morality, and to the rules of
> sound policy, to put an end to all traffick in the persons of
> men, and to the detention of their said persons in a state
> of slavery, as soon as the same may be effected without
> producing great inconveniences in the sudden change of
> practices of such long standing; and during the time of
> the continuance of the said practices, it is desirable and
> expedient, by proper regulations, to lessen the inconve-
> niences and evils attendant on the said traffick and state
> of servitude, until both shall be gradually done away . . .

Burke's prescriptions involve improving the conditions of slave ships so slaves would be better fed and clothed.[21] Regulations for proper treatment of Africans would be enforced by an attorney general in England with the title Protector of the Negroes.[22] He also wanted to create what amounted to English missions in Afri-ca, complete with churches, schools, and hospitals.[23] Burke's sketch strikes the modern reader as quaint and patronizing, but that need not render a poor judgment of his effort. The mainstream abolition-ist thought in the late 1700s was in favor of gradual abolition, and Burke's proposals induce reflection on the evilness of the practice and how to confine the practice and reduce its evilness. All such discourse and sentiment opened the way for abolishing the prac-tice altogether.

The "Sketch of the Negro Code" shows just how seriously Burke took reformation. It also shows his reluctance to change. He saw

---

21. Ibid., p. 262.

22. Ibid., p. 272.

23. Ibid., p. 265.

resolutions to the problem of slavery within the existing English legal system and constitutional order. While Burke's sketch was never adopted, England did take a gradual approach to abolition, first abolishing the slave trade and then slavery itself some years after, and all slaves in the British Isles were freed by a legal decision. Burke's faith in the English constitution was not ill-founded, as it eventually delivered abolition without war, unlike the United States.

Slavery was not the only area where Burke favored reform. He also supported Catholic emancipation. In "A Letter to Sir Hercules Langrishe," Burke makes a case for reform of the English laws that disenfranchised Catholics. In so doing, he makes it clear he is not changing anything; he is reforming in response to a grievance complained of. He appeals repeatedly to the English constitution, which "is not made for great, general, and proscriptive exclusions; sooner or later, it will destroy them, or they will destroy the constitution."[24]

The exclusion of Catholics from the franchise was one such exclusion. Burke writes, "I believe no man will assert seriously, that when people are of a turbulent spirit, the best way to keep them in order, is to furnish them with something substantial to complain of."[25] In keeping with his hurdles from the East India bill, he points out the magnitude of Catholic disenfranchisement: "The body of disenfranchised men will not be perfectly satisfied to remain always in that state. If they are not satisfied, you have two millions of subjects in your bosom, full of uneasiness."[26] An unruly mob is undesirable for society, and "lawful enjoyment is the surest method to prevent unlawful gratification."[27]

---

24. Ibid., p. 204.

25. Ibid., p. 229.

26. Ibid., p. 241.

27. Ibid., p. 207.

Burke goes to great lengths to demonstrate that Catholic enfranchisement is not in contradiction with any fundamental parts of the English constitution. He draws a distinction between fundamental and secondary laws:

> There is no man on earth, I believe, more willing than I am to lay it down as a fundamental of the constitution, that the church of England should be united and even identified with it: but allowing this, I cannot allow that all *laws of regulation*, made from time to time, in support of that fundamental law, are, of course, equally fundamental and equally unchangeable. . . . None of this species of *secondary and subsidiary laws* have been held fundamental. They have yielded to circumstances: particularly where they were thought, even in their consequences, or obliquely, to affect other fundamentals.[28]

Catholic exclusion is a secondary law, according to Burke. Since it was not a fundamental law, enfranchising Catholics was a response to a grievance complained of, and therefore was a reform, not a change. It was also a question of prudence.[29] Burke concludes the letter by saying Catholics should be enfranchised "for the stability of the church and state, and for the union and the separation of the people: for the union of the honest and peaceable of all sects; for their separation from all that is ill-intentioned and seditious in any of them."[30] Burke was not advocating changing the constitution, just reforming in the name of civic peace in accordance with longstanding constitutional principles.

28. Ibid., pp. 216-217. Italics in original.

29. Ibid., 239.

30. Ibid., 251.

Burke's support for reform in Indian affairs, slavery, and Catholic enfranchisement were liberalizing, but one might argue that Burke's efforts did not flow from any overriding liberal principles. His justifications, it might be said, were different in each case, and he doesn't see each reform as part of a coherent liberal plan of any sort. Burke erects a status quo presumption that is difficult to clear, and there are other cases in his writings where the presumption is not overcome. We, however, like many of today's leading Burke scholars, including Richard Bourke, Richard Whatmore, Gregory Collins, and Yuval Levin, think otherwise. Something like Adam Smith's natural liberty, or "the liberal plan," "allowing every man to pursue his own interest his own way,"[31] plays a role in Burke's political outlook, some would say a central role.[32]

Burke disdains the French revolutionaries and their enthusiasm for change. In *Reflections on the Revolution in France*, Burke investigates three of the revolutionaries' principles of government. One of them is "a right of cashiering their governors for *misconduct* [italics original]."[33] Burke argues that misconduct is far too low a hurdle: "No government could stand a moment, if it could be blown down with anything so loose and indefinite as an opinion of '*misconduct*'."[34] He writes in almost religious terms:

> To avoid therefore the evils of inconstancy and versatility, ten thousand times worse than those of obstinacy and

31. Adam Smith. 1976. *An Inquiry Into the Nature and Causes of The Wealth of Nations*, eds. R. H. Campbell and A. S. Skinner, 2 vols. Oxford: Oxford University Press., pp. 664, 687.

32. That the liberty principle plays a central role in Burke's political outlook is expounded by D.B. Klein, 2021, "Conservative Liberalism: Hume, Smith, and Burke as Policy Liberals and Polity Conservatives," *Journal of Economic Behavior and Organization* 183, pp. 861-873.

33. Edmund Burke, *Reflections on the Revolution in France*, Indianapolis: Liberty Fund, 1999, p. 114.

34. Ibid., 115. Italics in original.

the blindest prejudice, we have *consecrated* the state; that no man should approach to look into its defects or corruptions but with due caution; that he should never dream of beginning its reformation by its subversion; that he should approach to the faults of the state as to the wounds of a father, with pious awe and trembling solicitude.[35]

Altering something consecrated should require a high burden of proof, and Burke argues the French have not met that burden:

Your government in France, though usually, and I think justly, reputed the best of the unqualified or ill-qualified monarchies, was still full of abuses. . . . I am no stranger to the faults and defects of the subverted government of France; and I think I am not inclined by nature or policy to make a panegyric upon any thing which is a just and natural object of censure. But the question is not now of the vices of that monarchy, but of its existence. Is it then true, that the French government was such as to be incapable or undeserving of reform; so that it was of absolute necessity the whole fabric should be at once pulled down, and the area cleared for the erection of the theoretic experimental edifice in its place?[36]

In bringing up "the theoretic experimental edifice" the revolutionaries put in place of the monarchy, Burke is also asking the fundamental question, "Compared to what?" That question must weigh on the mind of any reformer. Not only did the revolutionaries not

35. Ibid., 192.

36. Ibid., pp. 226-227.

clear the requisite hurdles to justify reform, they didn't even put together a plan to resolve the (legitimate) grievances complained of.

On the issue of liberty, Burke expresses a view that is not common to our modern discussions on the topic. In his eyes, the French have not shown themselves qualified for liberty. He writes:

> Men are qualified for civil liberty, in exact proportion to their disposition to put moral chains upon their own appetites; in proportion as their love of justice is above their rapacity; in proportion as their soundness and sobriety of understanding is above their vanity and presumption; in proportion as they are more disposed to listen to the counsels of the wise and good, in preference to the flattery of knaves. Society cannot exist unless a controlling power upon will and appetite be placed somewhere, and the less of it there is within, the more there must be without. It is ordained in the eternal constitution of things, that men of intemperate minds cannot be free. Their passions forge their fetters.[37]

Contrasting Burke's harshness on the French with his compassion for the Indians and Africans is instructive. Burke excoriates the French for throwing off their "mild monarchy," saying they "murdered, robbed, and rebelled," using "the practices of incendiaries, assassins, housebreakers, robbers, spreaders of false news, forgers of false orders from authority, and other delinquencies, of which ordinary justice takes cognizance."[38] Not only were the French grievances insufficiently great in Burke's eyes, the French people's behavior has proven them unfit for liberty.

---

37. Ibid., 69.
38. Ibid., 70.

Their behavior was also a threat to the continent at large. In "Thoughts on French Affairs," Burke insists, "The present Revolution in France seems to me to be quite of another character and description . . . *It is a Revolution of doctrine and theoretick dogma.*"[39] The only other revolution like that in European history was the Reformation, which created terrible unrest. Burke sees the French Revolution in military terms, describing it as "an amazing conquest wrought by a change of opinion. . . . If early steps are not taken in some way or other to prevent the spreading of this influence, I scarcely think any [country] perfectly secure."[40] In *Letters on Regicide Peace*, Burke advocates a military solution, essentially a late eighteenth-century D-Day, anticipating support from a large portion of the French people, to liberate France from its Jacobin oppressors and restore monarchy. He certainly did not hold the pacifist beliefs many libertarians hold today.

"An Appeal from the Old to the New Whigs" gives insight into Burke's somewhat confusing thoughts on liberty. He makes a distinction between speaking in general and speaking in particular:

> I allow, as I ought to do, for the effusions which come from a *general* zeal for liberty. This is to be indulged, and even to be encouraged, as long as the *question is general*. An orator, above all men, ought to be allowed a full and free use of the praise of liberty. A common place in favour of slavery and tyranny delivered to a popular assembly, would indeed be a bold defiance to all the principles of rhetoric. But in a question whether any particular constitution is or is not a plan of rational liberty, this kind of rhetorical flourish in favour of freedom in gener-

---

39. Ibid., 208. Italics in original.

40. Ibid., 221.

al, is surely a little out of its place. It is virtually a begging of the question. It is a song of triumph, before the battle.[41]

Note the modifier on "liberty" when he's writing about particulars: "rational." Elsewhere Burke speaks of "*social* freedom,"[42] meaning freedom or liberty enjoyed in actual social existence. The French had not ordered their politics so as to augment liberty in actual social existence.

Burke writes, "When people see a political object, which they ardently desire . . . they are apt extremely to palliate, or underrate the evils which may arise in obtaining it. This is no reflection on the humanity of those persons. . . . It only shews that they are not sufficiently informed, or sufficiently considerate."[43] Burke, when he advocated reform, tried his best to be informed and considerate. He was one of the foremost experts in Parliament on affairs in India, and his "Sketch of the Negro Code" certainly considered many of the difficulties that reality presented. It was not for nothing that Burke was paid high tribute in Thomas Clarkson's famous 1808 history of the movement to abolish the slave-trade in Britain.[44]

Being well versed in metaphysics does not count as informed and considerate, however. Burke writes, "Nothing universal can be rationally affirmed on any moral, or any political subject. Pure metaphysical abstraction does not belong to these matters."[45] There are many exceptions to general principles that must be discerned

41. Ibid., 88. Italics in original.

42. Ritchie, (Letter to Charles-Jean-François Depont), p. 12

43. Ibid., 89.

44. Clarkson, Thomas. 1808. *The History of the Rise, Progress, & Accomplishment of the Abolition of the African Slave-trade, by the British Parliament,* 2 volumes. London: Longman, Hurst, Rees, and Orme.

45. Ritchie., p. 91.

with prudence. "Prudence is not only the first in rank of the virtues political and moral, but she is the director, the regulator, the standard of them all."[46] That cautious discernment extends to liberty itself: "Rational and experienced men, tolerably well know, and have always known, how to distinguish between true and false liberty."[47] Burke's "Appeal" can be read as an appeal that the Whigs not become a party of liberty fanatics, but instead support a practical and ordered liberty according to by-and-large presumptions, using prudence to discern exceptions.

Burke's clearest exposition of what he means by liberty is in his "Letter to Charles-Jean-François Depont." He at first seems to contradict what has already been discussed as to the universality of liberty, but then qualifies his statement and remains consistent with what he writes in the "Appeal" and elsewhere about the French. He writes:

> You hope, sir, that I think the French deserving of liberty.
> I certainly do. I certainly think that all men who desire it,
> deserve it. It is not the reward of our merit, or the acquisition of our industry. It is our inheritance. It is the birthright of our species. We cannot forfeit our right to it, but
> by what forfeits our title to the privileges of our kind. I
> mean the abuse, or oblivion, of our rational faculties, and
> a ferocious indocility which makes us prompt to wrong
> and violence, destroys our social nature, and transforms
> us into something little better than the description of
> wild beasts. To men so degraded, a state of strong constraint is a sort of necessary substitute for freedom; since,
> bad as it is, it may deliver them in some measure from the

---

46. Ibid.

47. Ibid., p. 198.

worst of all slavery—that is, the despotism of their own
blind and brutal passions.[48]

He models in his own rhetoric what he described in the "Appeal."
When he speaks of liberty generally, it is in glowing terms. When
he talks about a particular circumstance, however, when men
have abused their "rational faculties," he makes an exception. He
argues that a sort of despotism may be necessary to prevent a worse
despotism.

Burke writes that freedom:

> is not solitary, unconnected, individual, selfish liberty,
> as if every man was to regulate the whole of his con-
> duct by his own will. The liberty I mean is *social* free-
> dom. It is that state of things in which liberty is secured
> by the equality of restraint. A constitution of things in
> which the liberty of no one man, and no body of men,
> and no number of men, can find means to trespass on
> the liberty of any person, or any description of persons,
> in the society. This kind of liberty is, indeed, but another
> name for justice; ascertained by wise laws, and secured
> by well-constructed institutions.[49]

In Burke's liberty, everyone is restrained morally and politically
with the goal of social harmony. That view fits perfectly with his
advocacy of reform in India, abolition, and Catholic emancipation.
All three of those areas were the cause of great social discord in
Britain, and that irked Burke. They were impediments to freedom

---

48. Ibid., p. 7.

49. Ibid., pp. 7-8. Italics in orignal.

in ways that the existence of a monarchy is not. They were impediments to social freedom.

Poverty is itself a social bad, but it is also a threat to social freedom. Burke supported economic policy to make Britain prosper-
ous. He embraced the liberal economic thought most famously
expounded by Adam Smith. In Burke's most thorough work on
economics, "Thoughts and Details on Scarcity," he consistently
takes the liberal side of the economic argument. The piece as post-
humously presented is bookended by two clear statements in favor
of economic liberty in the name of poverty alleviation. His open-
ing sentence: "Of all things, an indiscreet tampering with the trade
of provisions is the most dangerous, and it is always worst in the
time when men are most disposed to it: that is, in the time of scarcity."[50] His closing sentence: "My opinion is against an over-doing
of any sort of administration, and more especially against this most
momentous of all meddling on the part of authority; the meddling
with the subsistence of the people."[51]

Those sentences frame the rest of the piece well. He writes
that government owes the public accurate information and "timely coercion," acting to restrain bad actors, not to "provide for us
in our necessities."[52] He views arbitrary taxation as unacceptable
coercion.[53] He talks of the concatenate coordination of economic
activity in a way much like Smith:

> The proposition is self-evident, and nothing but the malig-
> nity, perverseness, and ill-governed passions of mankind,
> and particularly the envy they bear to each other's pros-

---

50. Canavan, ed., *Miscellaneous Writings*, p. 61.

51. Ibid., p. 92.

52. Ibid.

53. Ibid., p. 65.

perity, could prevent their seeing and acknowledging it, with thankfulness to the benign and wise disposer of all things, who obliges men, whether they will or not, in pursuing their own selfish interests, to connect the general good with their own individual success.[54]

Burke is against "compulsory equalizations" because they "pull down what is above. They never raise what is below: and they depress high and low together beneath the level of what was originally the lowest."[55] Market prices are the best and only way to settle the "balance of wants" in society, and "they who wish the destruction of that balance, and would fain by arbitrary regulation decree, that defective production should not be compensated by encreased price, directly lay their *axe* to the root of production itself [italics original]."[56] "The moment the Government appears at market, all the principles of market will be subverted," and with that sentence, we can safely count Burke as a liberal on domestic economic policy. His economic thought was in line with Hume and Smith, and there was easy communication between them.

When it came to international trade, Burke was similarly liberal. He wrote two letters on trade with Ireland that advocated liberalization. At the time of Burke's writing, Ireland was a client state of Great Britain, but it was not united under the crown like Scotland, so there were still trade barriers between Ireland and Great Britain. At the beginning of the first letter, he lays out "liberality in the commercial system" between the two countries as the goal.[57] He argues trade is not zero-sum and that "England and Ireland may

---

54. Ibid., p. 67-68.

55. Ibid., p. 69.

56. Ibid., p. 77.

57. Ibid., p. 33.

flourish together. The world is large enough for us both."[58] Burke maintains his preference for gradual change in trade liberalization just like he does elsewhere, writing "it is a settled rule with me, to make the most of my *actual situation*; and not to refuse to do a proper thing, because there is something else more proper."[59]

His support for liberalization also arises from his observation of the experience of other countries; perhaps surprisingly, he singles out France, saying that despite France's large size, its many provinces "carry on trade and manufactures with perfect equality," and "all of them are properly poised and harmonised."[60] He is still cautious and observant of how the principles of liberal international trade actually work, not content to apply unpracticed theories. In the second letter, he bemoans that "we should consider those as rivals, whom we ought to regard as fellow-labourers in a common cause."[61] Burke's humane liberalism is scarcely better displayed than in that sentence. When it comes to international and domestic economics, there is no doubt as to Burke's liberalism.

Another important thing to remember about apparent contradictions in Burke's thought is his emphasis on circumstances, which will appear in many quotes throughout this book. His thought demonstrates the difference between being principled and being dogmatic. Principled people are committed to a way of interpreting the world, but they can acknowledge the circumstances and adjust accordingly. Dogmatic people are also committed to a way of interpreting the world, but they are unable to adjust as the circumstance calls.

Consider one of the impressive displays of duty-bound courage

---

58. Ibid., p. 37.

59. Ibid., p. 38. Italics in original.

60. Ibid.

61. Ibid., p. 46.

in recent history: New York City firefighters on September 11, 2001. The images of the World Trade Center towers burning after the airplanes struck are intense and can be interpreted in many different ways. Those various interpretations often depend on who someone is. Closeness to the event would dictate the intensity to the response. If you're a relative of someone who worked in the towers, you'd interpret those images as an attack on your family. If you're a New Yorker, you'd interpret them as an attack on your city. If you're an American, you'd interpret those images as an attack on your country. If you're all three of those, you'd have to juggle interpretations. Some interpretations are quite perverse: If you're a member of al-Qaeda, you'd interpret those images as a success.

Another way to say someone is duty-bound is to say they have been trained to commit to one interpretation over others. What made the New York City firefighters who went to the towers and began climbing the stairs so admirable was their commitment to one interpretation of the images of the attack: They interpreted it as a building on fire. When a building is on fire, they're trained to get to it as quickly as possible and put the fire out. The strength of will it took for them to sideline all other interpretations of the events and just see a building on fire is what makes their courage so remarkable. Deep down inside, they had to know that it would be unlikely they would be able to put the fire out. Deep down inside, they had to know many of them would not make it out alive. But they pressed on anyway because they had a duty to perform. They committed to one way of interpreting the world at a time when few other people would have.

Committing to one way of interpreting the world all the time, however, is dangerous, and this example is no exception. Let's say firefighters who survived were at an event on the fifth anniversary of the attacks to commemorate those who lost their lives. The firefighters see the same images of the burning towers five years later. In that context, it would be improper to just see a building on fire. It would be improper to sit in the audience at an event like that and think about firefighting strategy. Other interpretations are clearly superior in those circumstances.

Duty means committing to one interpretation of events at a time when many others wouldn't use that interpretation. But it doesn't mean being a one-track mind. That's the problem with dogmatic people. They can't adjust with the circumstances. Principled people have a sense of duty, but they also appreciate circumstances.

Burke felt he had a duty to his constituents, a duty to Britain, and a duty to humankind. He felt he had a duty to the present and a duty to the future. He felt he had a duty to liberty in policy and a duty to stability in polity. And most importantly, he knew when circumstances demanded that he use one interpretation of events over another. Burke was principled, not dogmatic. He believed the same things, but he had a steady hand on the dial to turn the intensity up or down as circumstances required.

***

It is with all that in mind that readers should take in the quotes in this book. Burke devoted the last years of his life to fighting against radicalism, dogmatism, and stubborn, foolish instincts. The radicalism we see today is not the product of left-wing universities, socialist intellectuals, or the Frankfurt School. It is not the product of any one country or any one culture. It is a product of human nature, and that hasn't changed since Burke put pen to paper. There is something natural about radicalism, and like other natural penchants, it must be overcome through training and education, through instituting of a complex, layered sense of duty. If this book helps to instill a sense of duty in its readers to defend liberal policy and stable polity like Burke did, it will have achieved its goal.

DANIEL B. KLEIN & DOMINIC PINO

Edmund Burke and the Perennial Battle, 1789-1797

Letter to Charles-Jean-François Depont
NOVEMBER 1789

You hope, sir, that I think the French deserving of liberty. I certainly do. I certainly think that all men who desire it, deserve it. It is not the reward of our merit, or the acquisition of our industry. It is our inheritance. It is the birthright of our species. (7)

Permit me . . . to tell you what the freedom is that I love, and that to which I think all men entitled. This is the more necessary, because, of all the loose terms in the world, liberty is the most indefinite. It is not solitary, unconnected, individual, selfish liberty, as if every man was to regulate the whole of his conduct by his own will. The liberty I mean is *social* freedom. It is that state of things in which liberty is secured by the equality of restraint. A constitution of things in which the liberty of no one man, and no body of men, and no number of men, can find means to trespass on the liberty of any person, or any description of persons, in the society. This kind of liberty is, indeed, but another name for justice; ascertained by wise laws, and secured by well-constructed institutions. I am sure that liberty, so incorporated, and in a manner identified with justice, must be infinitely dear to every one who is capable of conceiving what it is. But whenever a separation is made between liberty and justice, neither is, in my opinion, safe. I do not believe that men ever did submit, certain I am that they never ought to have submitted, to the arbitrary pleasure of one man; but, under circumstances in which the arbitrary pleasure of many persons in the community pressed with an intolerable hardship upon the just and equal rights of their fellows, such a choice might be made, as among evils. The moment *will* is set above reason and justice, in any community, a great question may arise in sober minds, in what part or portion of the community that dangerous dominion of *will* may be the least mischievously placed. (7-8)

You [the French] may have made a revolution, but not a reformation. You may have subverted monarchy, but not recovered freedom. (12)

You have theories enough concerning the rights of men; it may not be amiss to add a small degree of attention to their nature and disposition. (13)

[W]hen violent measures are in agitation, one ought to be pretty clear that there are no others to which we can resort, and that a predilection from character to such methods is not the true cause of their being proposed. The state was reformed by Sylla and by Caesar; but the Cornelian law and the Julian law were not worth the proscription. The pride of the Roman nobility deserved a check; but I cannot, for that reason, admire the conduct of Cinna, and Marius, and Saturninus. (14)

> [Lucius Cornelius Sulla Felix (138-78 BC), whom Burke refers to as "Sylla," was the first Roman leader to gain power in the Republic by force. Julius Caesar (100-44 BC) followed his example. By "the Cornelian law and the Julian law," Burke is referring to the constitutional changes made Sulla and Caesar. Cinna, Marius, and Saturninus were part of the Populares fac-

tion, which opposed Sulla's Optimates faction. The Optimates were seen as the conservative side, favoring the aristocratic order, so it's no surprise that Burke finds himself sympathetic to their cause.]

A positively vicious and abusive government ought to be changed– and, if necessary, by violence–if it cannot be (as sometimes it is the case) reformed. But when the question is concerning the more or the less *perfection* in the organization of a government, the allowance to *means* is not of so much latitude. There is, by the essential fundamental constitution of things, a radical infirmity in all human contrivances; and the weakness is often so attached to the very perfection of our political mechanism, that some defect in it–something that stops short of its principle, something that controls, that mitigates, that moderates it–becomes a necessary corrective to the evils that the theoretic perfection would produce. I am pretty sure it often is so; and this truth may be exemplified abundantly. (15)

[P]rudence... will lead us rather to acquiesce in some qualified plan, that does not come up to the full perfection of the abstract idea, than to push for the more perfect, which cannot be attained without tearing to pieces the whole contexture of the commonwealth, and creating a heart-ache in a thousand worthy bosoms. (15)

[P]erhaps a young man could not do better than to retreat for a while into study, to leave the field to those whose duty or inclination, or the necessities of their condition, have put them in possession of it, and wait for the settlement of such a commonwealth as an honest man may act in with satisfaction and credit. (17)

Reflections on the Revolution in France
1790

Circumstances (which with some gentlemen pass for nothing) give in reality to every political principle its distinguishing colour, and discriminating effect. The circumstances are what render every civil and political scheme beneficial or noxious to mankind . . . [C]ould I, in common sense, ten years ago, have felicitated France on her enjoyment of a government (for she then had a government [the *Ancien Régime*]) without enquiry what the nature of that government was, or how it was administered? (93)

[P]olitics and the pulpit are terms that have little agreement. No sound ought to be heard in the church but the healing voice of Christian charity. The cause of civil liberty and civil government gains as little as that of religion by this confusion of duties. Those who quit their proper character, to assume what does not belong to them, are, for the greater part, ignorant both of the character they leave, and of the character they assume. (97)

> [This comment was spurred by a sermon given by Richard Price (1723-1791), a preacher and political activist who supported the French Revolution.]

Surely the church is a place where one day's truce ought to be allowed to the dissensions and animosities of mankind. (97)

The propagators of this political gospel are in hopes their abstract principle (their principle that a popular choice is necessary to the legal existence of the sovereign magistracy) would be overlooked whilst the king of Great Britain was not affected by it. In the mean time the ears of their congregations would be gradually habituated to it, as if it were a first principle admitted without dispute. For the present it would only operate as a theory, pickled in the preserving juices of pulpit eloquence[.] (100)

It is far from impossible to reconcile, if we do not suffer ourselves to be entangled in the mazes of metaphysic sophistry, the use both of a fixed rule and an occasional deviation; the sacredness of an hereditary principle of succession in our government, with a power of change in its application in cases of extreme emergency. Even in that extremity (if we take the measure of our rights by our exercise of them at the Revolution) the change is to be confined to the peccant part only: to the part which produced the necessary deviation[.] (108)

The gentlemen of the Society for Revolutions see nothing in that of 1688 but the deviation from the constitution; and they take the deviation from the principle for the principle. (110)

> [The Society for Revolutions was a radical club in London that supported the French Revolution. Richard Price was a member. Burke's mention of 1688 refers to the Glorious Revolution, when William and Mary replaced James II on the English throne. William and Mary restored the powers of Parliament, which James had suspended, and the English Bill of Rights followed in 1689.]

[A]ll these considerations make it not unadviseable, in my opinion, to call back our attention to the true principles of our own domestic laws; that you, my French friend [the figurative audience of the *Reflections*], should begin to know, and that we should continue to cherish them. We ought not, on either side of the water, to suffer ourselves to be imposed upon by the counterfeit wares which some persons, by a double fraud, export to you in illicit bottoms as raw commodities of British growth, though wholly alien to our soil, in order afterwards to smuggle them back again into this country, manufactured after the newest Paris fashion of an improved liberty. (113)

The speculative line of demarcation, where obedience ought to end, and resistance must begin, is faint, obscure, and not easily definable. It is not a single act, or a single event, which determines it. Governments must be abused and deranged indeed, before it can be thought of; and the prospect of the future must be as bad as the experience of the past. When things are in that lamentable condition, the nature of the disease is to indicate the remedy to those whom nature has qualified to administer in extremities this critical, ambiguous, bitter potion to a distempered state. Times and occasions, and provocations, will teach their own lessons. The wise will determine from the gravity of the case; the irritable from sensibility to oppression; the high-minded from disdain and indignation at abusive power in unworthy hands; the brave and bold from the love of honourable danger in a generous cause; but, with or without right, a revolution will be the very last resource of the thinking and the good. (118-119)

Our oldest reformation is that of Magna Charta. You will see that Sir Edward Coke, that great oracle of our law, and indeed all the great men who follow him, to Blackstone, are industrious to prove the pedigree of our liberties. (119-120)

> [Edward Coke (1552-1634), pronounced "cook," was the pre-eminent English jurist before William Blackstone (1723-1780),

whose commentaries on English law are still influential today. Both were also judges.]

In the famous law of the 3rd of Charles I. called the Petition of Right, the parliament says to the king, "Your subjects have inherited this freedom," claiming their franchises, not on abstract principles as the "rights of men," but as the rights of Englishmen, and as a patrimony derived from their forefathers. (120)

> [The Petition of Right was passed in 1628 in response to Charles I violating property rights to fund his military. The Petition was introduced by Edward Coke. It can be seen as a step along the path to the English Bill of Rights.]

By a constitutional policy, working after the pattern of nature, we receive, we hold, we transmit our government and our privileges, in the same manner in which we enjoy and transmit our property and our lives. The institutions of policy, the goods of fortune, the gifts of Providence, are handed down, to us and from us, in the same course and order. Our political system is placed in a just correspondence and symmetry with the order of the world, and with the mode of existence decreed to a permanent body composed of transitory parts; wherein, by the disposition of a stupenduous wisdom, moulding together the great mysterious incorporation of the human race, the whole, at one time, is never old, or middle-aged, or young, but in a condition of unchangeable constancy, moves on through the varied tenour of perpetual decay, fall, renovation, and progression. Thus, by preserving the method of nature in the conduct of the state, in what we improve, we are never wholly new; in what we retain we are never wholly obsolete. By adhering in this manner and on those principles to our forefathers, we are guided

not by the superstition of antiquarians, but by the spirit of philosophic analogy. (122)

This idea of a liberal descent inspires us with a sense of habitual
native dignity, which prevents that upstart insolence almost inev-
itably adhering to and disgracing those who are the first acquir-
ers of any distinction. By this means our liberty becomes a noble
freedom. (123)

We procure reverence to our civil institutions on the principle upon
which nature teaches us to revere individual men; on account of
their age; and on account of those from whom they are descended.
All your sophisters cannot produce any thing better adapted to preserve a rational and manly freedom than the course that we have
pursued, who have chosen our nature rather than our speculations,
our breasts rather than our inventions, for the great conservatories
and magazines of our rights and privileges. (123)

[I]f diffident of yourselves, and not clearly discerning the almost
obliterated constitution of your ancestors, you [Burke's French
audience] had looked to your neighbours in this land [England],
who had kept alive the ancient principles and models of the old
common law of Europe meliorated and adapted to its present
state—by following wise examples you would have given new examples of wisdom to the world. You would have rendered the cause of
liberty venerable in the eyes of every worthy mind in every nation.
You would have shamed despotism from the earth, by showing
that freedom was not only reconcileable, but as, when well disciplined it is, auxiliary to law. You would have had an unoppressive
but a productive revenue. You would have had a flourishing commerce to feed it. You would have had a free constitution; a potent

monarchy; a disciplined army; a reformed and venerated clergy; a mitigated but spirited nobility, to lead your virtue, not to overlay it; you would have had a liberal order of commons, to emulate and to recruit that nobility; you would have had a protected, satisfied, laborious, and obedient people, taught to seek and to recognize the happiness that is to be found by virtue in all conditions; in which consists the true moral equality of mankind, and not in that monstrous fiction, which, by inspiring false ideas and vain expectations into men destined to travel in the obscure walk of laborious life, serves only to aggravate and imbitter that real inequality, which it never can remove; and which the order of civil life establishes as much for the benefit of those whom it must leave in an humble state, as those whom it is able to exalt to a condition more splendid, but not more happy. (125-126)

Nothing can secure a steady and moderate conduct in such assemblies, but that the body of them should be respectably composed, in point of condition in life, of permanent property, of education, and of such habits as enlarge and liberalize the understanding. (130)

[W]hen men are too much confined to professional and faculty habits, and, as it were, inveterate in the recurrent employment of that narrow circle, they are rather disabled than qualified for whatever depends on the knowledge of mankind, on experience in mixed affairs, on a comprehensive connected view of the various complicated external and internal interests which go to the formation of that multifarious thing called a state. (134)

To be attached to the subdivision, to love the little platoon we belong to in society, is the first principle (the germ as it were) of public affections. It is the first link in the series by which we proceed towards a love to our country and to mankind. (136)

There is no qualification for government, but virtue and wisdom, actual or presumptive. Wherever they are actually found, they have, in whatever state, condition, profession or trade, the passport of Heaven to human place and honour. Woe to the country which would madly and impiously reject the service of the talents and virtues, civil, military, or religious, that are given to grace and to serve it; and would condemn to obscurity every thing formed to diffuse lustre and glory around a state. Woe to that country too, that passing into the opposite extreme, considers a low education, a mean contracted view of things, a sordid mercenary occupation, as a preferable title to command. (140)

The power of perpetuating our property in our families is one of the most valuable and interesting circumstances belonging to it, and that which tends the most to the perpetuation of society itself. It makes our weakness subservient to our virtue; it grafts benevolence even upon avarice. The possessors of family wealth, and of the distinction which attends hereditary possession (as most concerned in it) are the natural securities for this transmission. With us, the house of peers is formed upon this principle. It is wholly composed of hereditary property and hereditary distinction; and made therefore the third of the legislature; and in the last event, the sole judge of all property in all its subdivisions. (142)

They [the French revolutionaries] have "the rights of men." Against these there can be no prescription; against these no agreement is binding: these admit no temperament, and no compromise: any thing withheld from their full demand is so much of fraud and injustice. Against these their rights of men let no government look for security in the length of its continuance, or in the justice and lenity of its administration. The objections of these speculatists, if its forms do not quadrate with their theories, are as valid against such an old and beneficent government as against the most violent tyranny, or the greenest usurpation. (149-150)

Far am I from denying in theory; full as far is my heart from withholding in practice, (if I were of power to give or to withhold,) the real rights of men. In denying their false claims of right, I do not mean to injure those which are real, and are such as their pretended rights would totally destroy. If civil society be made for the advantage of man, all the advantages for which it is made become his right. (150)

They have a right to the fruits of their industry; and to the means of making their industry fruitful. They have a right to the acquisitions of their parents; to the nourishment and improvement of their offspring; to instruction in life, and to consolation in death. Whatever each man can separately do, without trespassing upon others, he has a right to do for himself; and he has a right to a fair portion of all which society, with all its combinations of skill and force, can do in his favour. In this partnership all men have equal rights; but not to equal things. He that has but five shillings in the partnership, has as good a right to it, as he that has five hundred pound has to his larger proportion. But he has not a right to an equal dividend in the product of the joint stock; and as to the share of power, authority, and direction which each individual ought to have in the management of the state, that I must deny to be amongst the direct original rights of man in civil society; for I have in my con-

templation the civil social man, and no other. It is a thing to be settled by convention. (150-151)

[I]t is with infinite caution that any man ought to venture upon
pulling down an edifice which has answered in any tolerable degree
for ages the common purposes of society, or on building it up again,
without having models and patterns of approved utility before his
eyes. (153)

Hypocrisy, of course, delights in the most sublime speculations; for,
never intending to go beyond speculation, it costs nothing to have
it magnificent. But even in cases where rather levity than fraud was
to be suspected in these ranting speculations, the issue has been
much the same. These professors, finding their extreme principles
not applicable to cases which call only for a qualified, or, as I may
say, civil and legal resistance, in such cases employ no resistance
at all. It is with them a war or a revolution, or it is nothing. Finding their schemes of politics not adapted to the state of the world
in which they live, they often come to think lightly of all public
principle; and are ready, on their part, to abandon for a very trivial
interest what they find of very trivial value. (155-156)

[C]onsidering their speculative designs as of infinite value, and the
actual arrangement of the state as of no estimation, they are at best
indifferent about it. They see no merit in the good, and no fault in
the vicious management of public affairs; they rather rejoice in the
latter, as more propitious to revolution. They see no merit or demer-
it in any man, or any action, or any political principle, any further
than as they may forward or retard their design of change: they
therefore take up, one day, the most violent and stretched prerogative, and another time the wildest democratic ideas of freedom,

and pass from the one to the other without any sort of regard to cause, to person, or to party. (156)

The worst of these politics of revolution is this; they temper and harden the breast, in order to prepare it for the desperate strokes which are sometimes used in extreme occasions. (157)

This sort of people are so taken up with their theories about the rights of man, that they have totally forgot his nature. (157)

I hear, and I rejoice to hear, that the great lady [Marie Antoinette], the other object of the triumph, has borne that day (one is interested that beings made for suffering should suffer well) and that she bears all the succeeding days, that she bears the imprisonment of her husband [Louis XVI], and her own captivity, and the exile of her friends, and the insulting adulation of addresses, and the whole weight of her accumulated wrongs, with a serene patience, in a manner suited to her rank and race, and becoming the offspring of a sovereign distinguished for her piety and her courage [Maria Theresa of Austria]; that like her she has lofty sentiments; that she feels with the dignity of a Roman matron; that in the last extremity she will save herself from the last disgrace, and that if she must fall, she will fall by no ignoble hand. (169)

> [Burke was mocked by contemporaries for his tender veneration of the queen.]

It is now sixteen or seventeen years since I saw the queen of France, then the dauphiness, at Versailles; and surely never lighted on this orb, which she hardly seemed to touch, a more delightful vision. I saw her just above the horizon, decorating and cheering the elevated sphere she just began to move in; glittering like the morning star, full of life, and splendor, and joy. Oh! what a revolution! and what an heart must I have, to contemplate without emotion that elevation and that fall! Little did I dream when she added titles of veneration to those of enthusiastic, distant, respectful love, that she should ever be obliged to carry the sharp antidote against disgrace concealed in that bosom; little did I dream that I should have lived to see such disasters fallen upon her in a nation of gallant men, in a nation of men of honour and of cavaliers. I thought ten thousand swords must have leaped from their scabbards to avenge even a look that threatened her with insult. But the age of chivalry is gone. That of sophisters, oeconomists, and calculators, has succeeded; and the glory of Europe is extinguished for ever. Never, never more, shall we behold that generous loyalty to rank and sex, that proud submission, that dignified obedience, that subordination of the heart, which kept alive, even in servitude itself, the spirit of an exalted freedom. The unbought grace of life, the cheap defence of nations, the nurse of manly sentiment and heroic enterprize, is gone! It is gone, that sensibility of principle, that chastity of honour, which felt a stain like a wound, which inspired courage whilst it mitigated ferocity, which ennobled whatever it touched, and under which vice itself lost half its evil, by losing all its grossness. (169-170)

All the decent drapery of life is to be rudely torn off. All the superadded ideas, furnished from the wardrobe of a moral imagination, which the heart owns, and the understanding ratifies, as necessary to cover the defects of our naked shivering nature, and to raise it to dignity in our own estimation, are to be exploded as a ridiculous, absurd, and antiquated fashion. (171)

On this scheme of things, a king is but a man; a queen is but a woman; a woman is but an animal; and an animal not of the highest order. All homage paid to the sex in general as such, and without distinct views, is to be regarded as romance and folly. Regicide, and parricide, and sacrilege, are but fictions of superstition, corrupting jurisprudence by destroying its simplicity. The murder of a king, or a queen, or a bishop, or a father, are only common homicide; and if the people are by any chance, or in any way gainers by it, a sort of homicide much the most pardonable, and into which we ought not to make too severe a scrutiny. (171)

Nothing is left which engages the affections on the part of the commonwealth. On the principles of this mechanic philosophy, our institutions can never be embodied, if I may use the expression, in persons; so as to create in us love, veneration, admiration, or attachment. But that sort of reason which banishes the affections is incapable of filling their place. (171)

Kings will be tyrants from policy when subjects are rebels from principle. (172)

[O]ur manners, our civilization, and all the good things which are connected with manners, and with civilization, have, in this European world of ours, depended for ages upon two principles; and were indeed the result of both combined; I mean the spirit of a gentleman, and the spirit of religion. The nobility and the clergy, the one by profession, the other by patronage, kept learning in existence, even in the midst of arms and confusions, and whilst governments were rather in their causes than formed. (172-173)

Even commerce, and trade, and manufacture, the gods of our

oeconomical politicians, are themselves perhaps but creatures; are themselves but effects, which, as first causes, we choose to worship. They certainly grew under the same shade in which learning flourished. (173)

Already there appears a poverty of conception, a coarseness and vulgarity in all the proceedings of the assembly and of all their instructors. Their liberty is not liberal. Their science is presumptuous ignorance. Their humanity is savage and brutal. (174)

I have often been astonished, considering that we are divided from you but by a slender dyke of about twenty-four miles [the English Channel, which is 21 miles wide at its narrowest point and 150 miles wide at its widest], and that the mutual intercourse between the two countries has lately been very great, to find how little you seem to know of us. I suspect that this is owing to your forming a judgment of this nation from certain publications, which do very erroneously, if they do at all, represent the opinions and dispositions generally prevalent in England. The vanity, restlessness, petulance, and spirit of intrigue of several petty cabals, who attempt to hide their total want of consequence in bustle and noise, and puffing, and mutual quotation of each other, makes you imagine that our contemptuous neglect of their abilities is a mark of general acquiescence in their opinions. No such thing, I assure you. Because half a dozen grasshoppers under a fern make the field ring with their importunate chink, whilst thousands of great cattle, reposed beneath the shadow of the British oak, chew the cud and are silent, pray do not imagine, that those who make the noise are the only inhabitants of the field[.] (179-180)

Thanks to our sullen resistance to innovation, thanks to the cold sluggishness of our national character, we still bear the stamp of our forefathers. We have not, as I conceive, lost the generosity and dignity of thinking of the fourteenth century; nor as yet have we subtilized ourselves into savages. We are not the converts of Rousseau; we are not the disciples of Voltaire; Helvetius has made no progress amongst us. Atheists are not our preachers; madmen are not our lawgivers. We know that we have made no discoveries, and we think that no discoveries are to be made, in morality; nor many in the great principles of government, nor in the ideas of liberty, which were understood long before we were born, altogether as well as they will be after the grave has heaped its mould upon our presumption, and the silent tomb shall have imposed its law on our pert loquacity. In England we have not yet been completely embowelled of our natural entrails; we still feel within us, and we cherish and cultivate, those inbred sentiments which are the faithful guardians, the active monitors of our duty, the true supporters of all liberal and manly morals. (180-181)

> [Rousseau and Voltaire are familiar enough, but Helvetius has not had the same staying power. Claude Adrien Helvetius (1715-1771) wrote *De l'esprit*, which described his egoist philosophy and was written to oppose the thought of Montesquieu. Helvetius held strongly to "blank slate" philosophy and laid great stress on education or inculcation in the determination of a person's beliefs. In apparent agreement with Burke, Isaiah Berlin considered Helvetius an "enemy of freedom."]

[I]nstead of casting away all our old prejudices, we cherish them to a very considerable degree, and, to take more shame to ourselves, we cherish them because they are prejudices; and the longer they have lasted, and the more generally they have prevailed, the more we cherish them. We are afraid to put men to live and trade each on his own private stock of reason; because we suspect that this stock in each man is small, and that the individuals would do better to avail themselves of the general bank and capital of nations, and of ages. Many of our men of speculation, instead of exploding general prejudices, employ their sagacity to discover the latent wisdom which prevails in them. If they find what they seek, (and they seldom fail) they think it more wise to continue the prejudice, with the reason involved, than to cast away the coat of prejudice, and to leave nothing but the naked reason; because prejudice, with its reason, has a motive to give action to that reason, and an affection which will give it permanence. Prejudice is of ready application in the emergency; it previously engages the mind in a steady course of wisdom and virtue, and does not leave the man hesitating in the moment of decision, sceptical, puzzled, and unresolved. Prejudice renders a man's virtue his habit; and not a series of unconnected acts. Through just prejudice, his duty becomes a part of his nature. (182)

> [It is important to note that "prejudice" did not carry the same connotations when Burke was writing as it does today. Burke means any judgment one carries into a situation that influences behavior. Prejudices Burke might have in mind are reverence for the constitution, supporting the established church, or a presumption of liberty in making government policy.]

We know, and what is better, we feel inwardly, that religion is the basis of civil society, and the source of all good and of all comfort. In England we are so convinced of this, that there is no rust of superstition, with which the accumulated absurdity of the human mind might have crusted it over in the course of ages, that ninety-nine in an hundred of the people of England would not prefer to impiety. We shall never be such fools as to call in an enemy to the substance of any system to remove its corruptions, to supply its defects, or to perfect its construction. (185-186)

Violently condemning neither the Greek [Eastern Orthodox] nor the Armenian [Oriental Orthodox], nor, since heats are subsided, the Roman [Catholic] system of religion, we prefer the Protestant; not because we think it has less of the Christian religion in it, but because, in our judgment, it has more. We are protestants, not from indifference, but from zeal. (186)

We know, and it is our pride to know, that man is by his constitution a religious animal; that atheism is against, not only our reason, but our instincts; and that it cannot prevail long. But if, in the moment of riot, and in a drunken delirium from the hot spirit drawn out of the alembick [alembic, a still used for distillation] of hell, which in France is now so furiously boiling, we should uncover our nakedness by throwing off that Christian religion which has hitherto been our boast and comfort, and one great source of civilization amongst us, and among many other nations, we are apprehensive (being well aware that the mind will not endure a void) that some uncouth, pernicious, and degrading superstition, might take place of it. (186)

On these ideas, instead of quarrelling with establishments, as some do, who have made a philosophy and a religion of their hostility to such institutions, we cleave closely to them. We are resolved to keep an established church, an established monarchy, an established aristocracy, and an established democracy, each in the degree it exists, and in no greater. I shall shew you presently how much of each of these we possess ... It has been the misfortune, not as these gentlemen think it, the glory, of this age, that every thing is to be discussed; as if the constitution of our country were to be always a subject rather of altercation than enjoyment. (187)

First, I beg leave to speak of our church establishment, which is the first of our prejudices; not a prejudice destitute of reason, but involving in it profound and extensive wisdom. I speak of it first. It is first, and last, and midst in our minds. For, taking ground on that religious system, of which we are now in possession, we continue to act on the early received and uniformly continued sense of mankind. That sense not only, like a wise architect, hath built up the august fabric of states, but like a provident proprietor, to preserve the structure from prophanation and ruin, as a sacred temple, purged from all the impurities of fraud, and violence, and injustice, and tyranny, hath solemnly and for ever consecrated the commonwealth, and all that officiate in it. This consecration is made, that all who administer in the government of men, in which they stand in the person of God himself, should have high and worthy notions of their function and destination; that their hope should be full of immortality; that they should not look to the paltry pelf [money] of the moment, nor to the temporary and transient praise of the vulgar, but to a solid, permanent existence, in the permanent part of their nature, and to a permanent fame and glory, in the example they leave as a rich inheritance to the world. (187-188)

Such sublime principles ought to be infused into persons of exalted situations; and religious establishments provided, that may continually revive and enforce them. Every sort of moral, every sort of civil, every sort of politic institution, aiding the rational and natural ties that connect the human understanding and affections to the divine, are not more than necessary, in order to build up that wonderful structure, Man; whose prerogative it is, to be in a great degree a creature of his own making; and who when made as he ought to be made, is destined to hold no trivial place in the creation. But whenever man is put over men, as the better nature ought ever to preside, in that case more particularly, he should as nearly as possible be approximated to his perfection. (188)

All persons possessing any portion of power ought to be strongly and awefully impressed with an idea that they act in trust; and that they are to account for their conduct in that trust to the one great master, author and founder of society. (188)

But where popular authority is absolute and unrestrained ... [the electorate] are less under responsibility to one of the greatest controlling powers on earth, the sense of fame and estimation. The share of infamy that is likely to fall to the lot of each individual in public acts, is small indeed; the [corrective] operation of opinion being in the inverse ratio to the number of those who abuse power. Their own approbation of their own acts has to them the appearance of a public judgment in their favour. A perfect democracy is therefore the most shameless thing in the world. As it is the most shameless, it is also the most fearless. No man apprehends in his person he can be made subject to punishment. Certainly the people at large never ought: for as all punishments are for example towards the conservation of the people at large, the people at large can never become the subject of punishment by any human hand. It is therefore of infinite importance that they should not be suffered to imagine that their will, any more than that of kings, is the standard of right and wrong. They ought to be persuaded that they are full as little entitled, and far less qualified, with safety to themselves, to use any arbitrary power whatsoever; that therefore they are not, under a false shew of liberty, but, in truth, to exercise an unnatural inverted domination, tyrannically to exact, from those who officiate in the state, not an entire devotion to their interest, which is their right, but an abject submission to their occasional will; extinguishing thereby, in all those who serve them, all moral principle, all sense of dignity, all use of judgment, and all consistency of character, whilst by the very same process they give themselves up a proper, a suitable, but a most contemptible prey to the servile ambition of popular sycophants or courtly flatterers. (188-189)

By this unprincipled facility of changing the state as often, and as much, and in as many ways, as there are floating fancies or fashions, the whole chain and continuity of the commonwealth would be broken. No one generation could link with the other. Men would become little better than the flies of a summer. (191)

[T]he science of jurisprudence, the pride of the human intellect, which, with all its defects, redundancies, and errors, is the collected reason of ages, combining the principles of original justice with the infinite variety of human concerns, as a heap of old exploded errors, would be no longer studied [by the revolutionaries]. (191)

No principles [of property and law] would be early worked into the habits. As soon as the most able instructor had completed his laborious course of institution, instead of sending forth his pupil, accomplished in a virtuous discipline, fitted to procure him attention and respect, in his place in society, he would find everything altered; and that he had turned out a poor creature to the contempt and derision of the world, ignorant of the true grounds of estimation. Who would insure a tender and delicate sense of honour to beat almost with the first pulses of the heart, when no man could know what would be the test of honour in a nation, continually varying the standard of its coin? No part of life would retain its acquisitions. Barbarism with regard to science and literature, unskilfulness with regard to arts and manufactures, would infallibly succeed to the want of a steady education and settled principle; and thus the commonwealth itself would, in a few generations, crumble away, be disconnected into the dust and powder of individuality, and at length dispersed to all the winds of heaven. (192)

To avoid therefore the evils of inconstancy and versatility, ten thousand times worse than those of obstinacy and the blindest prejudice, we have consecrated the state; that no man should approach to look into its defects or corruptions but with due caution; that he should never dream of beginning its reformation by its subversion; that he should approach to the faults of the state as to the wounds of a father, with pious awe and trembling solicitude. (192)

Society is indeed a contract. Subordinate contracts, for objects of mere occasional interest, may be dissolved at pleasure; but the state ought not to be considered as nothing better than a partnership agreement in a trade of pepper and coffee, callico or tobacco, or some other such low concern, to be taken up for a little temporary interest, and to be dissolved by the fancy of the parties. It is to be looked on with other reverence; because it is not a partnership in things subservient only to the gross animal existence of a temporary and perishable nature. It is a partnership in all science; a partnership in all art; a partnership in every virtue, and in all perfection. As the ends of such a partnership cannot be obtained in many generations, it becomes a partnership not only between those who are living, but between those who are living, those who are dead, and those who are to be born. Each contract of each particular state is but a clause in the great primaeval contract of eternal society, linking the lower with the higher natures, connecting the visible and invisible world, according to a fixed compact sanctioned by the inviolable oath which holds all physical and all moral natures, each in their appointed place. This law is not subject to the will of those, who by an obligation above them, and infinitely superior, are bound to submit their will to that law. The municipal corporations of that universal kingdom are not morally at liberty at their pleasure, and on their speculations of a contingent improvement, wholly to separate and tear asunder the bands of their subordinate community, and to dissolve it into an unsocial, uncivil, unconnected chaos of elementary principles. (192-193)

These, my dear Sir, are, were, and I think long will be the sentiments of not the least learned and reflecting part of this kingdom. They who are included in this description ... conceive that He who gave our nature to be perfected by our virtue, willed also the necessary means of its perfection. He willed therefore the state; He willed its connexion with the source and original archetype of all perfection. They who are convinced of this his will, which is the law of laws and the sovereign of sovereigns, cannot think it reprehensible, that this our corporate fealty and homage, that this our recognition of a seigniory paramount, I had almost said this oblation of the state itself, as a worthy offering on the high altar of universal praise, should be performed, as all publick solemn acts are performed, in buildings, in musick, in decoration, in speech, in the dignity of persons, according to the customs of mankind, taught by their nature; that is, with modest splendour, with unassuming state, with mild majesty and sober pomp. For those purposes they think some part of the wealth of the country is as usefully employed, as it

can be in fomenting the luxury of individuals. It is the publick ornament. It is the publick consolation. It nourishes the publick hope.
The poorest man finds his own importance and dignity in it, whilst
the wealth and pride of individuals at every moment makes the man
of humble rank and fortune sensible of his inferiority, and degrades
and vilifies his condition. It is for the man in humble life, and to raise
his nature, and to put him in mind of a state in which the privileges
of opulence will cease, when he will be equal by nature, and may be
more than equal by virtue—that this portion of the general wealth
of his country is employed and sanctified. (194-195)

Our education is so formed as to confirm and fix this impression.
Our education is in a manner wholly in the hands of ecclesiastics, and in all stages from infancy to manhood. Even when our
youth, leaving schools and universities, enter that most important
period of life which begins to link experience and study together,
and when with that view they visit other countries, instead of old
domestics whom we have seen as governors to principal men from
other parts, three-fourths of those who go abroad with our young
nobility and gentlemen are ecclesiastics; not as austere masters,
nor as mere followers; but as friends and companions of a graver
character, and not seldom persons as well born as themselves. With
them, as relations, they most commonly keep up a close connexion through life. By this connexion we conceive that we attach our
gentlemen to the church; and we liberalize the church by an intercourse with the leading characters of the country. (196)

[W]e thought they [England's educational institutions] were susceptible of amendment, without altering the ground. We thought
that they were capable of receiving and meliorating, and above all
of preserving, the accessions of science and literature, as the order

of Providence should successively produce them. (197)

It is better to cherish virtue and humanity, by leaving much to free will, even with some loss to the object, than to attempt to make men mere machines and instruments of a political benevolence. The world on the whole will gain by a liberty, without which virtue cannot exist. (201)

But this act of seizure of property [the French revolutionary government seizing church property], it seems, is a judgment in law, and not a confiscation. They have, it seems, found out in the academies of the Palais Royal [a palace in Paris, whose gardens were a prominent meeting place], and the Jacobins, that certain men had no right to the possessions which they held under law, usage, the decisions of courts, and the accumulated prescription of a thousand years. They say that ecclesiastics are fictitious persons, creatures of the state; whom at pleasure they may destroy, and of course limit and modify in every particular; that the goods they possess are not properly theirs, but belong to the state which created the fiction; and we are therefore not to trouble ourselves with what they may suffer in their natural feelings and natural persons[.] (204)

They struck at the nobility through the crown and the church. They attacked them particularly on the side on which they thought them the most vulnerable, that is, the possessions of the church, which, through the patronage of the crown, generally devolved upon the nobility. The bishopricks, and the great commendatory abbies, were, with few exceptions, held by that order. (208)

The literary cabal had some years ago formed something like a regular plan for the destruction of the Christian religion. This object they pursued with a degree of zeal which hitherto had been discovered only in the propagators of some system of piety. They were possessed with a spirit of proselytism in the most fanatical degree; and from thence by an easy progress, with the spirit of persecution according to their means. What was not to be done towards their great end by any direct or immediate act, might be wrought by a longer process through the medium of opinion. To command that opinion, the first step is to establish a dominion over those who direct it . . . by endeavouring to confine the reputation of sense, learning, and taste to themselves or their followers. I will venture to say that this narrow, exclusive spirit has not been less prejudicial to literature and to taste, than to morals and true philosophy. (209)

A spirit of cabal, intrigue, and proselytism, pervaded all their thoughts, words, and actions. (210)

Writers, especially when they act in a body, and with one direction, have great influence on the publick mind; the alliance therefore of these writers with the monied interest had no small effect in removing the popular odium and envy which attended that species of wealth. These writers, like the propagators of all novelties, pretended to a great zeal for the poor, and the lower orders, whilst in their satires they rendered hateful, by every exaggeration, the faults of courts, of nobility, and of priesthood. They became a sort of demagogues. They served as a link to unite, in favour of one object, obnoxious wealth to restless and desperate poverty. (211)

As these two kinds of men [monied interests and political men of letters] appear principal leaders in all the late transactions, their junction and politics will serve to account, not upon any principles of law or of policy, but as a cause, for the general fury with which all the landed property of ecclesiastical corporations has been attacked[.] (211)

When the only estate lawfully possessed, and which the contracting parties had in contemplation at the time in which their bargain was made, happens to fail, who, according to the principles of natural and legal equity, ought to be the sufferer? Certainly it ought to be either the party who trusted; or the party who persuaded him to trust; or both; and not third parties who had no concern with the transaction. Upon any insolvency they ought to suffer who were weak enough to lend upon bad security, or they who fraudulently held out a security that was not valid. Laws are acquainted with no other rules of decision. But by the new institute of the rights of men, the only persons, who in equity ought to suffer, are the only persons who are to be saved harmless: those are to answer the debt who neither were lenders or borrowers, mortgagers or mortgagees. (212)

When all the frauds, impostures, violences, rapines, burnings, murders, confiscations, compulsory paper currencies, and every description of tyranny and cruelty employed to bring about and to uphold this revolution, have their natural effect, that is, to shock the moral sentiments of all virtuous and sober minds, the abettors of this philosophic system immediately strain their throats in a declamation against the old monarchical government of France. When they have rendered that deposed power sufficiently black, they then proceed in argument, as if all those who disapprove of their new abuses, must of course be partizans of the old; that those who reprobate their crude and violent schemes of liberty ought to be treated as advocates for servitude. (223)

Is it then a truth so universally acknowledged, that a pure democracy is the only tolerable form into which human society can be thrown, that a man is not permitted to hesitate about its merits, without the suspicion of being a friend to tyranny, that is, of being a foe to mankind? (224)

I do not know under what description to class the present ruling authority in France. It affects to be a pure democracy, though I think it in a direct train of becoming shortly a mischievous and ignoble oligarchy. (224)

In such a popular persecution, individual sufferers are in a much more deplorable condition than in any other. Under a cruel prince they have the balmy compassion of mankind to assuage the smart of their wounds; they have the plaudits of the people to animate their generous constancy under their sufferings: but those who are subjected to wrong under multitudes, are deprived of all external consolation. They seem deserted by mankind; overpowered by a conspiracy of their whole species. (225-226)

But steady independant minds, when they have an object of so serious a concern to mankind as government, under their contemplation, will disdain to assume the part of satirists and declaimers. They will judge of human institutions as they do of human characters. They will sort out the good from the evil, which is mixed in mortal institutions as it is in mortal men. (226)

Mr. Necker's book published in 1785, contains an accurate and interesting collection of facts relative to public oeconomy and to political arithmetic; and his speculations on the subject are in general wise and liberal. In that work he gives an idea of the state of France, very remote from the portrait of a country whose government was a perfect grievance, an absolute evil, admitting no cure but through the violent and uncertain remedy of a total revolution. (230)

> [Jacques Necker (1732-1804) was the French finance minister under Louis XVI. He published the state budget publicly for the first time in 1781 and was fired soon after. The book Burke references, *De l'Administration des Finances de la France*, was actually first published in 1784, and it is a treatise on law and economics.]

Causes thus powerful to acquire and to retain, cannot be found in discouraged industry, insecure property, and a positively destructive government. (231)

[W]hen I reflect on the excellence of her [France's] manufactures and fabrics, second to none but ours [England's], and in some particulars not second; when I contemplate the grand foundations of charity, public and private; when I survey the state of all the arts that beautify and polish life; when I reckon the men she has bred for extending her fame in war, her able statesmen, the multitude of her profound lawyers and theologians, her philosophers, her critics, her historians and antiquaries, her poets, and her orators sacred and profane, I behold in all this something which awes and commands the imagination, which checks the mind on the brink of precipitate and indiscriminate censure, and which demands, that we should very seriously examine, what and how great are the latent vices that could authorise us at once to level so spacious a fabric with the ground. I do not recognize, in this view of things, the despotism of Turkey. Nor do I discern the character of a government, that has been, on the whole, so oppressive, or so corrupt, or so negligent, as to be utterly unfit for all reformation. I must think such a government well deserved to have its excellencies heightened; its faults corrected; and its capacities improved into a British constitution. (232)

Whoever has examined into the proceedings of that deposed government for several years back, cannot fail to have observed, amidst the inconstancy and fluctuation natural to courts, an earnest endeavour towards the prosperity and improvement of the country; he must admit, that it had long been employed, in some instances, wholly to remove, in many considerably to correct, the abusive practices and usages that had prevailed in the state; and that even the unlimited power of the sovereign over the persons of his subjects, inconsistent, as undoubtedly it was, with law and liberty, had yet been every day growing more mitigated in the exercise. (232-233)

But if in point of prodigality in the expenditure of money, or in point of rigour in the exercise of power, it be compared with any of the former reigns, I believe candid judges will give little credit to the good intentions of those who dwell perpetually on the donations to favourites, or on the expences of the court, or on the horrors of the Bastile in the reign of Louis the XVIth. (233)

Whether the system, if it deserves such a name, now built on the ruins of that antient monarchy, will be able to give a better account of the population and wealth of the country, which it has taken under its care, is a matter very doubtful. . . . I hear that there are considerable emigrations from France; and that many, quitting that voluptuous climate, and that seductive Circean liberty, have taken refuge in the frozen regions, and under the British despotism, of Canada. (233)

["Circean liberty" is a reference to Homer's Odyssey, where
Circe, an enchantress who uses magical potions to turn people
into animals, seduces men with her beautiful voice and turns
them into her pets. By mentioning Canada in this way, Burke
seems to be referring to Quebec, where French speakers would
feel comfortable. Quebec was explored by Jacques Cartier and
was part of New France, but it was ceded to Britain after the
Seven Years' War in the 1763 Treaty of Paris.]

I shall always, however, consider that liberty as very equivocal in
her appearance, which has not wisdom and justice for her companions; and does not lead prosperity and plenty in her train. (235-236)

The advocates for this revolution, not satisfied with exaggerating
the vices of their antient government, strike at the fame of their
country itself, by painting almost all that could have attracted the
attention of strangers, I mean their nobility and their clergy, as
objects of horror. (236)

Read their instructions [that is, the privileged nobility's instruc-
tions] to their representatives. They breathe the spirit of liberty as
warmly, and they recommend reformation as strongly, as any other order. Their privileges relative to contribution were voluntarily
surrendered; as the king, from the beginning, surrendered all pre-
tence to a right of taxation. (237)

Upon a free constitution there was but one opinion in France. The
absolute monarchy was at an end. It breathed its last, without a
groan, without struggle, without convulsion. All the struggle, all
the dissension arose afterwards upon the preference of a despotic
democracy to a government of reciprocal controul. The triumph

of the victorious party was over the principles of a British constitution. (237)

I found your nobility for the greater part composed of men of an high spirit, and of a delicate sense of honour, both with regard to themselves individually, and with regard to their whole corps, over whom they kept, beyond what is common in other countries, a censorial eye. They were tolerably well bred; very officious, humane, and hospitable; in their conversation frank and open; with a good military tone; and reasonably tinctured with literature, particularly of the authors in their own language. Many had pretensions far above this description. I speak of those who were generally met with.

As to their behaviour to the inferior classes, they appeared to me to comport themselves towards them with good-nature, and with something more nearly approaching to familiarity, than is generally practised with us in the intercourse between the higher and lower ranks of life. (238-239)

Those of the commons, who approached to or exceeded many of the nobility in point of wealth, were not fully admitted to the rank and estimation which wealth, in reason and good policy, ought to bestow in every country; though I think not equally with that of other nobility. The two kinds of aristocracy were too punctiliously kept asunder ...

This separation, as I have already taken the liberty of suggesting to you, I conceive to be one principal cause of the destruction of the old nobility. The military, particularly, was too exclusively reserved for men of family. (240)

The strong struggle in every individual to preserve possession of what he has found to belong to him and to distinguish him, is one of the securities against injustice and despotism implanted in our nature. It operates as an instinct to secure property, and to preserve communities in a settled state. What is there to shock in this? Nobility is a graceful ornament to the civil order. It is the Corinthian capital of polished society. (241)

> [The Corinthian order is the most ornate order in classical architecture.]

It was with the same satisfaction I found that the result of my enquiry concerning your clergy was not dissimilar. It is no soothing news to my ears, that great bodies of men are incurably corrupt. It is not with much credulity I listen to any, when they speak evil of those whom they are going to plunder. I rather suspect that vices are feigned or exaggerated, when profit is looked for in their punishment. An enemy is a bad witness: a robber is a worse. Vices and abuses there were undoubtedly in that order [the clergy], and must be. It was an old establishment, and not frequently revised. But I saw no crimes in the individuals that merited confiscation of their substance, nor those cruel insults and degradations, and that unnatural persecution which has been substituted in the place of meliorating regulation. (241-242)

They find themselves obliged to rake into the histories of former ages (which they have ransacked with a malignant and profligate industry) for every instance of oppression and persecution which has been made by that body or in its favour, in order to justify, upon very iniquitous, because very illogical principles of retaliation, their own persecutions, and their own cruelties. After destroying all other genealogies and family distinctions, they invent a sort of pedigree of crimes. It is not very just to chastise men for the offences of their natural ancestors; but to take the fiction of ancestry in a corporate succession, as a ground for punishing men who have no relation to guilty acts, except in names and general descriptions, is a sort of refinement in injustice belonging to the philosophy of this enlightened age. The assembly punishes men, many, if not most, of whom abhor the violent conduct of ecclesiastics in former times as much as their present persecutors can do[.] (242)

Corporate bodies are immortal for the good of the members, but not for their punishment. Nations themselves are such corporations. As well might we in England think of waging inexpiable war upon all Frenchmen for the evils which they have brought upon us in the several periods of our mutual hostilities. You might, on your part, think yourselves justified in falling upon all Englishmen on account of the unparalleled calamities brought upon the people of France by the unjust invasions of our Henries and our Edwards. Indeed we should be mutually justified in this exterminatory war upon each other, full as much as you are in the unprovoked persecution of your present countrymen, on account of the conduct of men of the same name in other times. (242-243)

> [Henries and Edwards, indeed. Henry I invaded Normandy in the early twelfth century. Henry II fought many battles in France in the mid twelfth century. Henry III invaded France in 1230. Edward I held a duchy in France, which was the source of diplomatic conflict and rumors of wars. Edward II waged the War of Saint-Sardos against France in 1324. Edward III started the Hundred Years' War by claiming the French throne in 1337. He invaded Normandy, sacked Caen, and won the Battle of Crécy. That war continued through Henry IV's reign. Henry V inflamed the war, besieging Harfleur and famously winning the Battle of Agincourt in 1415 – he died near Paris in 1422. Hen-

ry VI was crowned King of France in 1431, with the Hundred
Years' War still ongoing. His reign was interrupted by Nor-
mandy-born Edward IV, who would also succeed him. Henry VII allied with Brittany against France. Henry VIII invad-
ed France in 1513 and again in 1544. The only ones who didn't
cause trouble in France were Edward V, who was only king for
a few months before his death at age 12, and Edward VI, who
reigned for six years and died at age 15.]

If there was in France, as in other countries there visibly is, a great
abatement, rather than any increase of these vices, instead of load-
ing the present clergy with the crimes of other men, and the odi-
ous character of other times, in common equity they ought to be
praised, encouraged, and supported, in their departure from a spirit which disgraced their predecessors, and for having assumed a
temper of mind and manners more suitable to their sacred function. (248)

I found the clergy in general, persons of moderate minds and dec-
orous manners; I include the seculars, and the regulars of both sex-
es. I had not the good fortune to know a great many of the paro-
chial clergy; but in general I received a perfectly good account of
their morals, and of their attention to their duties. With some of
the higher clergy I had a personal acquaintance; and of the rest in
that class, very good means of information. They were, almost all
of them, persons of noble birth. They resembled others of their own
rank; and where there was any difference, it was in their favour.
They were more fully educated than the military noblesse; so as
by no means to disgrace their profession by ignorance, or by want
of fitness for the exercise of their authority. They seemed to me,
beyond the clerical character, liberal and open; with the hearts of

gentlemen, and men of honour; neither insolent nor servile in their manners and conduct. (248-249)

["Seculars" are ordained Catholic clergy who do not belong to a particular order or institute. "Regulars" are ordained Catholic clergy who do.]

[T]his new ecclesiastical establishment is intended only to be temporary, and preparatory to the utter abolition, under any of its forms, of the Christian religion, whenever the minds of men are prepared for this last stroke against it, by the accomplishment of the plan for bringing its ministers into universal contempt. They who will not believe, that the philosophical fanatics who guide in these matters, have long entertained such a design, are utterly ignorant of their character and proceedings. These enthusiasts do not scruple to avow their opinion, that a state can subsist without any religion better than with one; and that they are able to supply the place of any good which may be in it, by a project of their own—namely, by a sort of education they have imagined, founded in a knowledge of the physical wants of men; progressively carried to an enlightened self-interest, which, when well understood, they tell us will identify with an interest more enlarged and public. The scheme of this education has been long known. Of late they distinguish it (as they have got an entire new nomenclature of technical terms) by the name of a Civic Education. (251-252, note: The LF volume does not use italics on "Civic Education" but the Yale volume does)

The teachers who reformed our religion in England bore no sort of resemblance to your present reforming doctors in Paris. Perhaps they were (like those whom they opposed) rather more than could be wished under the influence of a party spirit; but they were most sincere believers; men of the most fervent and exalted piety; ready to die, as some of them did die, like true heroes in defence of their particular ideas of Christianity; as they would with equal fortitude, and more chearfully, for that stock of general truth, for the branches of which they contended with their blood. These men would have disavowed with horror those wretches who claimed a fellowship with them upon no other titles than those of their having pillaged the persons with whom they maintained controversies, and their having despised the common religion, for the purity of which they exerted themselves with a zeal, which unequivocally bespoke their highest reverence for the substance of that system which they wished to reform. (252-254)

There are in England abundance of men who tolerate in the true spirit of toleration. They think the dogmas of religion, though in different degrees, are all of moment; and that amongst them there is, as amongst all things of value, a just ground of preference. They favour, therefore, and they tolerate. They tolerate, not because they despise opinions, but because they respect justice. They would reverently and affectionately protect all religions, because they love and venerate the great principle upon which all agree, and the great object to which they are all directed. They begin more and more plainly to discern, that we have all a common cause, as against a common enemy. They will not be so misled by the spirit of faction, as not to distinguish what is done in favour of their subdivision, from those acts of hostility, which, through some particular description, are aimed at the whole corps, in which they themselves, under another denomination, are included. (254)

With the national assembly of France, possession is nothing; law and usage are nothing. I see the national assembly openly reprobate the doctrine of prescription, which one of the greatest of their own lawyers [Jean Domat] tells us, with great truth, is a part of the law of nature. He tells us, that the positive ascertainment of its limits, and its security from invasion, were among the causes for which civil society itself has been instituted. If prescription be once shaken, no species of property is secure, when it once becomes an object large enough to tempt the cupidity of indigent power. (255)

When the Anabaptists of Münster, in the sixteenth century, had filled Germany with confusion by their system of levelling and their wild opinions concerning property, to what country in Europe did not the progress of their fury furnish just cause of alarm? Of all things, wisdom is the most terrified with epidemical fanaticism, because of all enemies it is that against which she is the least able to furnish any kind of resource. (257)

> [A radical group of Anabaptists in the German city of Münster took over the city government in 1534 and abolished private property. The leaders of the takeover were executed in 1536, and their bodies were put in cages and hung from the church tower.]

Many parts of Europe are in open disorder. In many others there is a hollow murmuring under ground; a confused movement is felt, that threatens a general earthquake in the political world. Already confederacies and correspondences of the most extraordinary nature are forming, in several countries. In such a state of things we ought to hold ourselves upon our guard. (260)

But it will be argued, that this confiscation [of church property] in France ought not to alarm other nations. They say it is not made from wanton rapacity; that it is a great measure of national policy, adopted to remove an extensive, inveterate, superstitious mischief. It is with the greatest difficulty that I am able to separate policy from justice. Justice is itself the great standing policy of civil society; and any eminent departure from it, under any circumstances, lies under the suspicion of being no policy at all. (260)

When men are encouraged to go into a certain mode of life by the existing laws, and protected in that mode as in a lawful occupation–when they have accommodated all their ideas, and all their habits to it–when the law had long made their adherence to its rules a ground of reputation, and their departure from them a ground of disgrace and even of penalty–I am sure it is unjust in legislature, by an arbitrary act, to offer a sudden violence to their minds and their feelings; forcibly to degrade them from their state and condition, and to stigmatize with shame and infamy that character and those customs which before had been made the measure of their happiness and honour. If to this be added an expulsion from their habitations, and a confiscation of all their goods, I am not sagacious enough to discover how this despotic sport, made of the feelings, consciences, prejudices, and properties of men, can be discriminated from the rankest tyranny. (260-261)

If the injustice of the course pursued in France be clear, the policy of the measure, that is, the public benefit to be expected from it, ought to be at least as evident, and at least as important. (261)

A man full of warm speculative benevolence may wish his society otherwise constituted than he finds it; but a good patriot, and a true politician, always considers how he shall make the most of the existing materials of his country. A disposition to preserve, and an ability to improve, taken together, would be my standard of a statesman. Every thing else is vulgar in the conception, perilous in the execution. (261-262)

There are moments in the fortune of states when particular men are called to make improvements by great mental exertion. In those moments, even when they seem to enjoy the confidence of their prince and country, and to be invested with full authority, they have not always apt instruments. A politician, to do great things, looks for a power, what our workmen call a purchase [leverage]; and if he finds that power, in politics as in mechanics he cannot be at a loss to apply it. (262)

In the monastic institutions, in my opinion, was found a great power for the mechanism of politic benevolence. There were revenues with a public direction; there were men wholly set apart and dedicated to public purposes, without any other than public ties and public principles; men without the possibility of converting the estate of the community into a private fortune; men denied to self-interests, whose avarice is for some community; men to whom personal poverty is honour, and implicit obedience stands in the place of freedom. In vain shall a man look to the possibility of making such things when he wants them. The winds blow as they list. These institutions are the products of enthusiasm; they are the instruments of wisdom. Wisdom cannot create materials; they are the gifts of nature or of chance; her pride is in the use. The perennial existence of bodies corporate and their fortunes, are things particularly suited to a man who has long views; who meditates designs that require time in fashioning; and which propose duration when they are accomplished. (262)

Your politicians do not understand their trade; and therefore they sell their tools. (263)

But the institutions savour of superstition in their very principle; and they nourish it by a permanent and standing influence. This I do not mean to dispute; but this ought not to hinder you from deriving from superstition itself any resources which may thence be furnished for the public advantage. You derive benefits from many dispositions and many passions of the human mind, which are of as doubtful a colour in the moral eye, as superstition itself. It was your business to correct and mitigate every thing which was noxious in this passion, as in all the passions. But is superstition the greatest of all possible vices? In its possible excess I think it becomes a very great evil. It is, however, a moral subject; and of course admits of all degrees and all modifications. Superstition is the religion of feeble minds; and they must be tolerated in an intermixture of it, in some trifling or some enthusiastic shape or other, else you will deprive weak minds of a resource found necessary to the strongest. The body of all true religion consists, to be sure, in obedience to the will of the sovereign of the world; in a confidence in his declarations; and an imitation of his perfections. The rest is our own. It may be prejudicial to the great end; it may be auxiliary. Wise men, who as such are not admirers, (not admirers at least of the Munera Terrae [mundane parts of life]) are not violently attached to these things, nor do they violently hate them. Wisdom is not the most severe corrector of folly. (263-264)

[I]f, in the contention between fond attachment and fierce antipathy concerning things in their nature not made to produce such heats, a prudent man were obliged to make a choice of what errors and excesses of enthusiasm he would condemn or bear, perhaps he would think the superstition which builds, to be more tolerable than that which demolishes; that which adorns a country, than that which deforms it; that which endows, than that which plunders; that which disposes to mistaken beneficence, than that which stimulates to real injustice; that which leads a man to refuse to himself lawful pleasures, than that which snatches from others the scanty subsistence of their self-denial. Such, I think, is very nearly the state of the question between the ancient founders of monkish superstition, and the superstition of the pretended philosophers of the hour. (264)

Why should the expenditure of a great landed property, which is a dispersion of the surplus product of the soil, appear intolerable to you or to me, when it takes its course through the accumulation of vast libraries, which are the history of the force and weakness of the human mind; through great collections of antient records, medals, and coins, which attest and explain laws and customs; through paintings and statues, that, by imitating nature, seem to extend the limits of creation; through grand monuments of the dead, which continue the regards and connexions of life beyond the grave; through collections of the specimens of nature, which become a representative assembly of all the classes and families of the world, that by disposition facilitate, and, by exciting curiosity, open the avenues to science? If, by great permanent establishments, all these objects of expence are better secured from the inconstant sport of personal caprice and personal extravagance, are they worse than if the same tastes prevailed in scattered individuals? (266-267)

Does not the sweat of the mason and carpenter, who toil in order to partake the sweat of the peasant, flow as pleasantly and as salubriously, in the construction and repair of the majestic edifices of religion, as in the painted booths and sordid sties of vice and luxury; as honourably and as profitably in repairing those sacred works, which grow hoary with innumerable years, as on the momentary receptacles of transient voluptuousness; in opera-houses, and brothels; and gaming-houses, and club-houses, and obelisks in the Champ de Mars? . . . Are the decorations of temples an expenditure less worthy a wise man than ribbons, and laces, and national cockades, and petits maisons, and petit soupers, and all the innumerable fopperies and follies in which opulence sports away the burthen of its superfluity? (267)

[W]hy proscribe the other [that is, the pious or devout works], and surely, in every point of view, the more laudable use of estates? Why, through the violation of all property, through an outrage upon every principle of liberty, forcibly carry them from the better to the worse? (267-268)

Those whose principle it is to despise the antient permanent sense of mankind, and to set up a scheme of society on new principles, must naturally expect that such of us who think better of the judgment of the human race than of theirs, should consider both them and their devices, as men and schemes upon trial. They must take it for granted that we attend much to their reason, but not at all to their authority. They have not one of the great influencing prejudices of mankind in their favour. They avow their hostility to opinion. Of course they must expect no support from that influence, which, with every other authority, they have deposed from the seat of its jurisdiction. (269-270)

I can never consider this assembly [the National Constituent Assembly, which lasted through September 1791] as any thing else than a voluntary association of men, who have availed themselves of circumstances, to seize upon the power of the state.... They do not hold the authority they exercise under any constitutional law of the state.... The most considerable of their acts have not been done by great majorities; and in this sort of near divisions, which carry only the constructive authority of the whole, strangers will consider reasons as well as resolutions. (270)

If they had set up this new experimental government as a necessary substitute for an expelled tyranny, mankind would anticipate the time of prescription, which, through long usage, mellows into legality governments that were violent in their commencement. All those who have affections which lead them to the conservation of civil order would recognize, even in its cradle, the child as legitimate, which has been produced from those principles of cogent expediency to which all just governments owe their birth, and on which they justify their continuance. But they will be late and reluctant in giving any sort of countenance to the operations of a power, which has derived its birth from no law and no necessity; but which on the contrary has had its origin in those vices and sinister practices by which the social union is often disturbed and sometimes destroyed. This assembly has hardly a year's prescription. We have their own word for it that they have made a revolution. To make a revolution is a measure which, prima fronte, requires an apology. To make a revolution is to subvert the antient state of our country; and no common reasons are called for to justify so violent a proceeding. The sense of mankind authorizes us to examine into the mode of acquiring new power, and to criticise on the use that is made of it, with less awe and reverence than that which is usually conceded to a settled and recognized authority. (270-271)

[T]hey commit the whole to the mercy of untried speculations; they abandon the dearest interests of the public to those loose theories, to which none of them would chuse to trust the slightest of his private concerns. They make this difference, because in their desire of obtaining and securing power they are thoroughly in earnest; there they travel in the beaten road. The public interests, because about them they have no real solicitude, they abandon wholly to chance; I say to chance, because their schemes have nothing in experience to prove their tendency beneficial. (271-272)

We must always see with a pity not unmixed with respect, the errors of those who are timid and doubtful of themselves with regard to points wherein the happiness of mankind is concerned. But in these gentlemen there is nothing of the tender parental solicitude which fears to cut up the infant for the sake of an experiment. (272)

I confess myself unable to find out any thing which displays, in a single instance, the work of a comprehensive and disposing mind, or even the provisions of a vulgar prudence. Their purpose every where seems to have been to evade and slip aside from difficulty. (272)

[I]t has been the glory of the great masters in all the arts to confront, and to overcome; and when they had overcome the first difficulty, to turn it into an instrument for new conquests over new difficulties; thus to enable them to extend the empire of their science; and even to push forward beyond the reach of their original thoughts, the land marks of the human understanding itself. Difficulty is a severe instructor, set over us by the supreme ordinance of a parental guardian and legislator, who knows us better than we know ourselves, as he loves us better too ... He that wrestles with us strengthens our nerves, and sharpens our skill. Our antagonist is our helper. This amicable conflict with difficulty obliges us to an intimate acquaintance with our object, and compels us to consider it in all its relations. (272-273)

It will not suffer us to be superficial. It is the want of nerves of understanding for such a task; it is the degenerate fondness for tricking short-cuts, and little fallacious facilities, that has in so many parts of the world created governments with arbitrary powers. They have created the late arbitrary monarchy of France. They have created the arbitrary republic of Paris. With them defects in wisdom are to be supplied by the plenitude of force. They get nothing by it. Commencing their labours on a principle of sloth, they have the common fortune of slothful men. The difficulties which they rather had eluded than escaped, meet them again in their course; they multiply and thicken on them; they are involved, through a labyrinth of confused detail, in an industry without limit, and without direction; and, in conclusion, the whole of their work becomes feeble, vitious, and insecure. (273)

It is this inability to wrestle with difficulty which has obliged the arbitrary assembly of France to commence their schemes of reform with abolition and total destruction. But is it in destroying and pulling down that skill is displayed? Your mob can do this as well at least as your assemblies. The shallowest understanding, the rudest hand, is more than equal to that task. Rage and phrenzy will pull down more in half an hour, than prudence, deliberation, and foresight can build up in an hundred years. The errors and defects of old establishments are visible and palpable. It calls for little ability to point them out; and where absolute power is given, it requires but a word wholly to abolish the vice and the establishment together. The same lazy but restless disposition, which loves sloth and hates quiet, directs these politicians, when they come to work, for supplying the place of what they have destroyed. To make every thing the reverse of what they have seen is quite as easy as to destroy. No difficulties occur in what has never been tried. Criticism is almost baffled in discovering the defects of what has not existed; and eager enthusiasm, and cheating hope, have all the wide field of imagination in which they may expatiate with little or no opposition. (273-274)

At once to preserve and to reform is quite another thing. When the useful parts of an old establishment are kept, and what is superadded is to be fitted to what is retained, a vigorous mind, steady persevering attention, various powers of comparison and combination, and the resources of an understanding fruitful in expedients are to be exercised; they are to be exercised in a continued conflict with the combined force of opposite vices; with the obstinacy that rejects all improvement, and the levity that is fatigued and disgusted with every thing of which it is in possession. (274)

The true lawgiver ought to have an heart full of sensibility. He ought to love and respect his kind, and to fear himself. It may be allowed to his temperament to catch his ultimate object with an intuitive glance; but his movements towards it ought to be deliberate. Political arrangement, as it is a work for social ends, is to be only wrought by social means. There mind must conspire with mind. Time is required to produce that union of minds which alone can produce all the good we aim at. Our patience will achieve more than our force. (275)

I have never yet seen any plan which has not been mended by the observations of those who were much inferior in understanding to the person who took the lead in the business. By a slow but well-sustained progress, the effect of each step is watched[.] (275)

We are enabled to unite into a consistent whole the various anomalies and contending principles that are found in the minds and affairs of men. From hence arises, not an excellence in simplicity, but one far superior, an excellence in composition. (276)

To proceed in this manner, that is, to proceed with a presiding principle, and a prolific energy, is with me the criterion of profound wisdom. (276)

Your legislators seem to have taken their opinions of all professions, ranks, and offices, from the declamations and buffooneries of satirists; who would themselves be astonished if they were held to the letter of their own descriptions. By listening only to these, your leaders regard all things only on the side of their vices and faults, and view those vices and faults under every colour of exaggeration. It is undoubtedly true, though it may seem paradoxical; but in general, those who are habitually employed in finding and displaying faults, are unqualified for the work of reformation: because their minds are not only unfurnished with patterns of the fair and good, but by habit they come to take no delight in the contemplation of those things. By hating vices too much, they come to love men too little. (276-277)

Mr. Hume told me, that he had from Rousseau himself the secret of his principles of composition. That acute, though eccentric, observer had perceived, that to strike and interest the public, the marvelous must be produced; that the marvellous of the heathen mythology had long since lost its effect; that giants, magicians, fairies, and heroes of romance which succeeded, had exhausted the portion of credulity which belonged to their age; that now nothing was left to a writer but that species of the marvellous, which might still be produced, and with as great an effect as ever, though in another way; that is, the marvellous in life, in manners, in characters, and in extraordinary situations, giving rise to new and unlooked-for strokes in politics and morals. (277-278)

It is remarkable, that in a great arrangement of mankind, not one reference whatsoever is to be found to any thing moral or any thing politic; nothing that relates to the concerns, the actions, the passions, the interests of men. (290)

It is impossible not to observe, that in the spirit of this geometrical distribution, and arithmetical arrangement, these pretended citizens treat France exactly like a country of conquest. Acting as conquerors, they have imitated the policy of the harshest of that harsh race. The policy of such barbarous victors, who contemn a subdued people, and insult their feelings, has ever been, as much as in them lay, to destroy all vestiges of the antient country, in religion, in polity, in laws, and in manners; to confound all territorial limits; to produce a general poverty; to put up their properties to auction; to crush their princes, nobles, and pontiffs; to lay low every thing which had lifted its head above the level, or which could serve to combine or rally, in their distresses, the disbanded people, under the standard of old opinion. They have made France free in the manner in which those sincere friends to the rights of mankind, the Romans, freed Greece, Macedon, and other nations. They destroyed the bonds of their union, under colour of providing for the independence of each of their cities. (291)

> [The revolutionaries in France had a plan to redraw the political subdivisions in the country based on a grid system that ignored all historical and geographical boundaries.]

When the members who compose these new bodies of cantons, communes, and departments ... begin to act, they will find themselves, in a great measure, strangers to one another. The electors and elected throughout, especially in the rural cantons, will be frequently without any civil habitudes or connections, or any of that natural discipline which is the soul of a true republic. Magistrates and collectors of revenue are now no longer acquainted with their districts, bishops with their dioceses, or curates with their parishes. These new colonies of the rights of men bear a strong resemblance to that sort of military colonies which Tacitus has observed upon in the declining policy of Rome. (291)

As the first sort of legislators attended to the different kinds of citizens, and combined them into one commonwealth, the others, the metaphysical and alchemistical legislators, have taken the direct contrary course. They have attempted to confound all sorts of citizens, as well as they could, into one homogeneous mass; and then they divided this their amalgama into a number of incoherent republics. They reduce men to loose counters merely for the sake of simple telling, and not to figures whose power is to arise from their place in the table. (293)

[E]very such classification, if properly ordered, is good in all forms of government; and composes a strong barrier against the excesses of despotism, as well as it is the necessary means of giving effect and permanence to a republic. For want of something of this kind, if the present project of a republic should fail, all securities to a moderated freedom fail along with it; all the indirect restraints which mitigate despotism are removed[.] (294)

[I]f monarchy should ever again obtain an entire ascendency in France, under this or under any other dynasty, it will probably be, if no voluntarily tempered at setting out, the most completely arbitrary power that has ever appeared on earth. (294)

Industry must wither away. Oeconomy must be driven from your country. Careful provision will have no existence. Who will labour without knowing the amount of his pay? Who will study to encrease what none can estimate? who will accumulate, when he does not know the value of what he saves? (303)

All these considerations leave no doubt on my mind, that if this monster of a constitution can continue, France will be wholly governed by the agitators in corporations, by societies in the towns formed of directors of assignats, and trustees for the sale of church lands, attornies, agents, money-jobbers, speculators, and adventurers, composing an ignoble oligarchy founded on the destruction of the crown, the church, the nobility, and the people. Here end all the deceitful dreams and visions of the equality and rights of men.

The other divisions of the kingdom being hackled and torn to pieces, and separated from all their habitual means, and even principles of union, cannot, for some time at least, confederate against her. Nothing was to be left in all the subordinate members, but weakness, disconnection, and confusion. (306)

It is boasted, that the geometrical policy has been adopted, that all local ideas should be sunk, and that the people should no longer be Gascons, Picards, Bretons, Normans, but Frenchmen, with one country, one heart, and one assembly. But instead of being all Frenchmen, the greater likelihood is, that the inhabitants of that region will shortly have no country. No man ever was attached by a sense of pride, partiality, or real affection, to a description of square measurement. He never will glory in belonging to the Checquer, No. 71, or to any other badge-ticket. We begin our public affections in our families. No cold relation is a zealous citizen. We pass on to our neighbourhoods, and our habitual provincial connections. These are inns and resting-places. Such divisions of our country as have been formed by habit, and not by a sudden jerk of authority, were so many little images of the great country in which the heart found something which it could fill. (307)

> [The "geometrical policy" is again the grid system of political
> subdivisions the revolutionaries proposed.]

The love to the whole is not extinguished by this subordinate partiality. Perhaps it is a sort of elemental training to those higher and more large regards, by which alone men come to be affected, as with their own concern, in the prosperity of a kingdom so extensive as that of France. (307)

Your all-sufficient legislators, in their hurry to do every thing at once, have forgot one thing that seems essential, and which, I believe, never has been before, in the theory or the practice, omitted by any projector of a republic. They have forgot to constitute a Senate, or something of that nature and character. Never, before this time, was heard of a body politic composed of one legislative and active assembly, and its executive officers, without such a council; without something to which foreign states might connect themselves; something to which, in the ordinary detail of government, the people could look up; something which might give a bias and steadiness and preserve something like consistency in the proceedings of state. Such a body kings generally have as a council. A monarchy may exist without it; but it seems to be in the very essence of a republican government. It holds a sort of middle place between the supreme power exercised by the people, or immediately delegated from them, and the mere executive. (308)

[A] political executive magistracy, though merely such, is a great trust. It is a trust indeed that has much depending upon its faithful and diligent performance, both in the person presiding in it and in all his subordinates. Means of performing this duty ought to be given by regulation; and dispositions towards it ought to be infused by the circumstances attendant on the trust. It ought to be environed with dignity, authority, and consideration, and it ought to lead to glory. The office of execution is an office of exertion. (310)

Executive magistracy ought to be constituted in such a manner, that those who compose it should be disposed to love and to venerate those whom they are bound to obey. (311)

Kings, even such as are truly kings, may and ought to bear the freedom of subjects that are obnoxious to them. They may too, without derogating from themselves, bear even the authority of such persons if it promotes their service. Louis the XIIIth mortally hated the cardinal de Richlieu; but his support of that minister against his rivals was the source of all the glory of his reign, and the solid foundation of his throne itself. Louis the XIVth, when come to the throne, did not love the cardinal Mazarin; but for his interests he preserved him in power. When old, he detested Louvois; but for years, whilst he faithfully served his greatness, he endured his person. When George the IId took Mr. Pitt, who certainly was not agreeable to him, into his councils, he did nothing which could humble a wise sovereign. But these ministers, who were chosen by affairs, not by affections, acted in the name of, and in trust for, kings; and not as their avowed, constitutional, and ostensible masters. (311)

[Louis XIII (1601-1643) became king at age nine. His mother was regent. Even when he became older, he relied on advisors to govern. Foremost among them was Cardinal Richelieu, who is responsible for much of the centralization of power in France, which might be what Burke refers to as "the solid foundation of his throne." Upon the death of Louis XIII, Louis XIV (1638-1715) became king at age four. He would reign 72 years and complete the centralization of power begun under his predecessor. Cardinal Mazarin (1602-1661) was his chief advisor early in his reign, and he was a very effective statesman. Louvois (1641-1691) was Louis XIV's war minister from 1662 until Louvois' death, and from 1683 on was also chief advisor. Conspicuously absent from Burke's account here is Jean-Baptiste Colbert (1619-1683), who was chief advisor to Louis XIV from 1661-1683 and is seen as the father of mercantilism in economics. Onto the British: George II (1683-1760) was king from 1727 until his death. Britain at that time was already fairly well established as a constitutional monarchy, with Parliament holding much of the power. Burke's "Mr. Pitt" is William Pitt the Elder (1708-1778), whom George II reluctantly appointed to the ministry to shore up support from Parliament. Pitt oversaw British victory in the Seven Years' War and eventually became prime minister.]

If you expect such obedience, amongst your other innovations and regenerations, you ought to make a revolution in nature, and provide a new constitution for the human mind. Otherwise, your supreme government cannot harmonize with its executory system. There are cases in which we cannot take up with names and abstractions. You may call half a dozen leading individuals, whom we have reason to fear and hate, the nation. It makes no other difference, than to make us fear and hate them the more. (312)

Whatever is supreme in a state, ought to have, as much as possible, its judicial authority so constituted as not only to depend upon it, but in some sort to balance it. It ought to give a security to its justice against its power. It ought to make its judicature, as it were, something exterior to the state. (317)

These parliaments had furnished, not the best certainly but some considerable corrective to the excesses and vices of the monarchy. Such an independent judicature was ten times more necessary when a democracy became the absolute power of the country. (317-318)

The vice of the antient democracies, and one cause of their ruin, was, that they ruled, as you do, by occasional decrees, psephismata [day-to-day policies in ancient Rome]. This practice soon broke in upon the tenour and consistency of the laws; it abated the respect of the people towards them; and totally destroyed them in the end. (319)

> [Burke is being a little dramatic here – there were many reasons for the fall of Rome.]

These administrative bodies are the great instruments of the present leaders in their progress through democracy to oligarchy. They must therefore be put above the law. (321)

> [The revoluntionaries supported vesting many powers that were previously in the monarchy in administrative bodies separate from the National Assembly.]

In the weakness of one kind of authority, and in the fluctuation of all, the officers of an army will remain for some time mutinous and full of faction, until some popular general, who understands the art of conciliating the soldiery, and who possesses the true spirit of command shall draw the eyes of all men upon himself. Armies will obey him on his personal account. There is no other way of securing military obedience in this state of things. But the moment in which that event shall happen, the person who really commands the army is your master; the master (that is little) of your king, the master of your assembly, the master of your whole republic. (332)

> [This is Burke's clearest prediction in the *Reflections* of the rise of someone like Napoleon Bonaparte.]

Every thing depends upon the army in such a government as yours; for you have industriously destroyed all the opinions, and prejudices, and, as far as in you lay, all the instincts which support government. (334)

The colonies assert to themselves an independent constitution and a free trade. They must be constrained by troops. In what chapter of your code of the rights of men are they able to read, that it is a part of the rights of men to have their commerce monopolized and restrained for the benefit of others? As the colonists rise on you, the negroes rise on them. Troops again—Massacre, torture, hanging! These are your rights of men! These are the fruits of metaphysic declarations wantonly made, and shamefully retracted! (335)

> [By the time of Burke's writing, much of France's North American empire was gone, with only Louisiana remaining. France still had significant holdings in the Caribbean, and in 1791, Burke's prediction in this quote came true when the slaves revolted in the colony of Saint Domingue, in modern-day Haiti. Toussaint Louverture (1743-1803) led that rebellion, which began the Haitian Revolution. The Haitian Revolution ended in 1804 with the establishment of Haiti as an independent country. After the revolution concluded, Haitians massacred thousands of Frenchmen who remained in the country. The defeat was a huge embarrassment for France.]

The [French] peasants, in all probability, are the descendants of these antient proprietors, Romans or Gauls. But if they fail, in any degree, in the titles which they make on the principles of antiquaries and lawyers, they retreat into the citadel of the rights of men. There they find that men are equal; and the earth, the kind and equal mother of all, ought not to be monopolized to foster the pride and luxury of any men, who by nature are no better than themselves, and who, if they do not labour for their bread, are worse. They find, that by the laws of nature the occupant and subduer of the soil is the true proprietor; that there is no prescription against nature. . . . As to the title by succession, they will tell you, that the succession of those who have cultivated the soil is the true pedigree of property, and not rotten parchments and silly substitutions[.] (336-337)

When the [French] peasants give you [the revolutionaries] back that coin of sophistic reason, on which you have set your image and superscription, you cry it down as base money, and tell them you will pay for the future with French guards, and dragoons, and hussars. (337)

> [Burke is continuing to emphasize what he sees as the inevitable militarization of the revolution. The French Guards were an elite unit under the *Ancien Régime* who defected from the King and were part of the storming of the Bastille. Dragoons and hussars are different kinds of cavalry.]

They have left nothing but their own arbitrary pleasure to determine what property is to be protected and what subverted. (339)

The people of Lyons, it seems, have refused lately to pay taxes. Why should they not? What lawful authority is there left to exact them? The king imposed some of them. The old states, methodised by orders, settled the more antient. They may say to the assembly, Who are you, that are not our kings, nor the states we have elected, nor sit on the principles on which we have elected you? And who are we, that when we see the gabelles, which you have ordered to be paid, wholly shaken off, when we see the act of disobedience afterwards ratified by yourselves—who are we, that we are not to judge what taxes we ought or ought not to pay, and who are not to avail ourselves of the same powers, the validity of which you have approved in others? To this the answer is, We will send troops. The last reason of kings is always the first with your assembly. (339)

> [The city of Lyon is currently the third-largest in France, and at the time of the Revolution, it was the second-largest. As a large city located over 250 miles from Paris, Lyon tried to assert itself during the Revolution. There were tax riots in 1789

and 1790, which is what Burke is referencing here. Burke's pre-
diction of troops came true: Revolutionary armies laid siege to
Lyon in 1793 after a rebellion broke out.]

The assembly keep a school where, systematically, and with unre-
mitting perseverance, they teach principles, and form regulations,
destructive to all spirit of subordination, civil and military—and
then they expect that they shall hold in obedience an anarchic
people by an anarchic army! (339-340)

I wish my countrymen rather to recommend to our neighbours
the example of the British constitution, than to take models from
them for the improvement of our own. In the former they have got
an invaluable treasure. They are not, I think, without some causes of apprehension and complaint; but these they do not owe to
their constitution, but to their own conduct. I think our happy situation owing to our constitution; but owing to the whole of it, and
not to any part singly; owing in a great measure to what we have
left standing in our several reviews and reformations, as well as to
what we have altered or superadded. Our people will find employment enough for a truly patriotic, free, and independent spirit, in
guarding what they possess, from violation. I would not exclude
alteration neither; but even when I changed, it should be to preserve. I should be led to my remedy by a great grievance. In what
I did, I should follow the example of our ancestors. I would make
the reparation as nearly as possible in the style of the building. A
politic caution, a guarded circumspection, a moral rather than a
complexional timidity, were among the ruling principles of our
forefathers in their most decided conduct. Not being illuminated
with the light of which the gentlemen of France tell us they have
got so abundant a share, they acted under a strong impression of

the ignorance and fallibility of mankind. He that had made them thus fallible, rewarded them for having in their conduct attended to their nature. Let us imitate their caution, if we wish to deserve their fortune, or to retain their bequests. Let us add, if we please; but let us preserve what they have left; and, standing on the firm ground of the British constitution, let us be satisfied to admire rather than attempt to follow in their desperate flights the aëronauts of France. (363-364)

I have told you candidly my sentiments. I think they are not likely to alter yours. I do not know that they ought. You are young; you cannot guide, but must follow the fortune of your country. But hereafter they may be of some use to you, in some future form which your commonwealth may take. In the present it can hardly remain; but before its final settlement it may be obliged to pass, as one of our poets says, "through great varieties of untried being," and in all its transmigrations to be purified by fire and blood. (364)

I have little to recommend my opinions, but long observation and much impartiality. They come from one who has been no tool of power, no flatterer of greatness; and who in his last acts does not wish to [belie] the tenour of his life. They come from one, almost the whole of whose public exertion has been a struggle for the liberty of others; from one in whose breast no anger durable or vehement has ever been kindled, but by what he considered as tyranny; and who snatches from his share in the endeavours which are used by good men to discredit opulent oppression, the hours he has employed on your affairs; and who in so doing persuades himself he has not departed from his usual office. They come from one who desires honours, distinctions, and emoluments, but little, and who expects them not at all; who has no contempt for fame,

and no fear of obloquy; who shuns contention, though he will hazard an opinion: from one who wishes to preserve consistency; but
who would preserve consistency by varying his means to secure the
unity of his end; and, when the equipoise of the vessel in which he
sails may be endangered by overloading it upon one side, is desir-
ous of carrying the small weight of his reasons to that which may
preserve its equipoise. (364-365)

A Letter to a Member of the National Assembly
MAY 1791

Can false political principles be more effectually exposed, than by
demonstrating that they lead to consequences directly inconsistent
with and subversive of the arrangements grounded upon them? (32)

There is no safety for honest men, but by believing all possible evil
of evil men, and by acting with promptitude, decision, and steadiness on that belief. (33)

The Assembly recommends to its youth a study of the bold experi-
menters in morality. Every body knows that there is a great dispute
amongst their leaders, which of them is the best resemblance to
Rousseau. In truth, they all resemble him. His blood they transfuse
into their minds and into their manners. Him they study; him they
meditate; him they turn over in all the time they can spare from
the laborious mischief of the day, or the debauches of the night.
Rousseau is their canon of holy writ; in his life he is their canon of
Polycletus; he is their standard figure of perfection. To this man
and this writer, as a pattern to authors and to Frenchmen, the

founderies of Paris are now running for statues, with the kettles of their poor and the bells of their churches ... It is impossible, therefore, putting the circumstances together, to mistake their design in choosing the author, with whom they have begun to recommend a course of studies. (47-48)

> [Burke was not a fan of Jean-Jacques Rousseau (1712-1778) of Geneva, the philosopher influential in France whose body the revolutionary government moved to Paris' Pantheon in 1794.]

True humility, the basis of the Christian system, is the low, but deep and firm foundation of all real virtue. (48)

When your lords had many writers as immoral as the object of their statue (such as Voltaire and others) they chose Rousseau; because in him that peculiar vice which they wished to erect into a ruling virtue, was by far the most conspicuous. (48)

[T]hey erect statues to a wild, ferocious, low-minded, hard-hearted father, of fine general feelings; a lover of his kind, but a hater of his kindred. (50)

> [Burke is referencing statues of Rousseau.]

[I] n their system of changing your manners to accommodate them to their politics, they found nothing so convenient as Rousseau. (52)

I am certain that the writings of Rousseau lead directly to this kind of shameful evil. I have often wondered how he comes to be so much more admired and followed on the continent than he is here.... We cannot rest upon any of his works, though they contain observations which occasionally discover a considerable insight into human nature. But his doctrines, on the whole, are so inapplicable to real life and manners, that we never dream of drawing from them any rule for laws or conduct, or for fortifying or illustrating any thing by a reference to his opinions. (53)

The great object of your tyrants, is to destroy the gentlemen of France; and for that purpose they destroy, to the best of their power, all the effect of those relations which may render considerable men powerful or even safe. To destroy that order, they vitiate the whole community. That no means may exist of confederating against their tyranny, by the false sympathies of this Nouvelle Eloise [a book by Rousseau], they endeavour to subvert those principles of domestic trust and fidelity, which form the discipline of social life. (54)

They destroy all the tranquillity and security of domestic life; turning the asylum of the house into a gloomy prison, where the father of the family must drag out a miserable existence, endangered in proportion to the apparent means of his safety; where he is worse than solitary in a croud of domestics, and more apprehensive from his servants and inmates, than from the hired blood-thirsty mob without doors, who are ready to pull him to the lanterne [alluding to the iron bracket of a lamppost used as a makeshift gallows]. (54)

Your despots govern by terror. They know, that he who fears God fears nothing else; and therefore they eradicate from the mind, through their Voltaire, their Helvetius, and the rest of that infamous gang, that only sort of fear which generates true courage. Their object is, that their fellow citizens may be under the dominion of no awe, but that of their committee of research, and of their lanterne. (55)

[Claude Adrien Helvetius (1715-1771) was a French writer
famous for his response to Montesquieu and espousal of blank-
slate philosophy.]

They, whose known policy it is to assassinate every citizen whom
they suspect to be discontented by their tyranny, and to corrupt the
soldiery of every open enemy, must look for no modified hostility.
All war, which is not battle, will be military execution. This will
beget acts of retaliation from you; and every retaliation will beget
a new revenge. The hell-hounds of war, on all sides, will be uncou-
pled and unmuzzled. The new school of murder and barbarism,
set up in Paris, having destroyed (so far as in it lies) all the other
manners and principles which have hitherto civilized Europe, will
destroy also the mode of civilized war, which, more than any thing
else, has distinguished the Christian world. (55-56)

Plans must be made for men. We cannot think of making men, and
binding nature to our designs. (63)

What a number of faults have led to this multitude of misfortunes,
and almost all from this one source, that of considering certain
general maxims, without attending to circumstances, to times, to
places, to conjunctures, and to actors! If we do not attend scrupu-
lously to all these, the medicine of to-day becomes the poison of
to-morrow. (65)

When I praised the British constitution, and wished it to be well
studied, I did not mean that its exterior form and positive arrangement should become a model for you, or for any people servilely to
copy. I meant to recommend the *principles* from which it has grown,

and the policy on which it has been progressively improved out of elements common to you and to us. (65)

The wretched scheme of your present masters [the French revolutionaries], is not to fit the constitution to the people, but wholly to destroy conditions, to dissolve relations, to change the state of the nation, and to subvert property, in order to fit their country to their theory of a constitution. (69)

Men are qualified for civil liberty, in exact proportion to their disposition to put moral chains upon their own appetites; in proportion as their love to justice is above their rapacity; in proportion as their soundness and sobriety of understanding is above their vanity and presumption; in proportion as they are more disposed to listen to the counsels of the wise and good, in preference to the flattery of knaves. (69)

An Appeal from the New to the Old Whigs
AUGUST 1791

[In this work, Burke refers to himself in the third-person. He defends himself against claims of inconsistency. He says the Whigs have changed, not he. His "appeal" is like appealing one's case from one court to another: He wishes to have his case transferred from the court of the New Whigs, now corrupted and hostile to Burke, to the court of the Old Whigs, those circa the time of and following the Glorious Revolution.]

[T]his fictitious majority [in France] had fabricated a constitution, which as now it stands, is a tyranny far beyond any example that can be found in the civilized European world of our age; [and] therefore the lovers of it must be lovers, not of liberty, but, if they really understand its nature, of the lowest and basest of all servitude. (83)

[I]t is not, an undigested, imperfect, and crude scheme of liberty, which may gradually be mellowed and ripened into an orderly and social freedom; but ... is so fundamentally wrong, as to be utterly incapable of correcting itself by any length of time, or of being formed into any mode of polity ... (83)

[The French revolutionaries'] new persecution is not against a variety in conscience, but against all conscience.... [I]t professes contempt towards its object; and whilst it treats all religion with scorn, is not so much as neutral about the modes: It unites the opposite evils of intolerance and of indifference. (84)

[T]heir ultimate violence arose from their original fraud. (84)

I allow, as I ought to do, for the effusions which come from a *general* zeal for liberty. This is to be indulged, and even to be encouraged, as long as the *question is general*. An orator, above all men, ought to be allowed a full and free use of the praise of liberty. A common place in favour of slavery and tyranny delivered to a popular assembly, would indeed be a bold defiance to all the principles of rhetoric. But in [touting a new] particular constitution [as] a plan of rational liberty, this kind of rhetorical flourish in favour of freedom in general, is surely a little out of its place. It is virtually a begging of the question. It is a song of triumph, before the battle. (88)

Nothing universal can be rationally affirmed on any moral, or any political subject. Pure metaphysical abstraction does not belong to these matters. The lines of morality are not like the ideal lines of mathematics. They are broad and deep as well as long. They admit of exceptions; they demand modifications. These exceptions and modifications are not made by the process of logic, but by the rules of prudence. (91)

[Burke here refers to himself in the third-person:]

Mr. Burke, since the publication of his pamphlet, has been a thousand times charged in the news-papers with holding despotic principles. He could not enjoy one moment of domestic quiet, he could not perform the least particle of public duty, if he did not altogether disregard the language of those libels. But however his sensibility might be affected by such abuse, it would in him have been thought a most ridiculous reason for shutting up the mouths of Mr. Fox, or Mr. Sheridan, so as to prevent their delivering their sentiments of the French revolution, that forsooth, "the news-papers had lately charged Mr. Burke with being an enemy to liberty." (97)

[Charles James Fox (1749-1806) was leader of the Whig faction that Burke was going after in this work. Burke and Fox were initially friends, but they became bitter enemies over their different views of the French Revolution. Richard Brinsley Sheridan (1751-1816) was a playwright and poet who also served in Parliament as a more radical Whig. He was firmly on Fox's side in the debate over the French Revolution, and broke with Burke very early on.]

[Burke sets the burden of proof for overcoming the presumption
of liberty pretty low, so that he may *sustain* the burden-level that
he sets:]

[Mr. Burke] told the House, upon an important occasion, and pretty early in his service, that "being warned by the ill effect of a contrary procedure in great examples, he had taken his ideas of liberty
very low; in order that they should stick to him, and that he might
stick to them to the end of his life." (104)

The liberty to which Mr. Burke declared himself attached, is not
French liberty. That liberty is nothing but the rein given to vice
and confusion. (105)

[Burke reviews Burke on American affairs:]

They contended, that the Americans had from the beginning aimed
at independence; that from the beginning they meant wholly to
throw off the authority of the crown, and to break their connec-
tion with the parent country. This Mr. Burke never believed. (106)

[Mr. Burke] always firmly believed that they were purely on the
defensive in that rebellion. He considered the Americans as standing at that time, and in that controversy, in the same relation to
England, as England did to king James the Second, in 1688 [during
the Glorious Revolution]. He believed, that they had taken up arms
from one motive only; that is our attempting to tax them without
their consent; to tax them for the purposes of maintaining civil and
military establishments. (107)

Considering the Americans on that defensive footing, [Mr. Burke]
thought Great Britain ought instantly to have closed with them

by the repeal of the taxing act. He was of opinion that our general rights over that country would have been preserved by this timely concession.When, instead of this, a Boston port bill, a Massachuset's charter bill, a Fishery bill, an Intercourse bill, I know not how many hostile bills rushed out like so many tempests from all points of the compass, and were accompanied first with great fleets and armies of English, and followed afterwards with great bodies of foreign troops, he thought that their cause grew daily better, because daily more defensive; and that ours, because daily more offensive, grew daily worse. He therefore in two motions, in two successive years, proposed in parliament many concessions beyond what he had reason to think in the beginning of the troubles would ever be seriously demanded.

So circumstanced, he certainly never could and never did wish the colonists to be subdued by arms. He was fully persuaded, that if such should be the event, they must be held in that subdued state by a great body of standing forces, and perhaps of foreign forces. He was strongly of opinion, that such armies, first victorious over Englishmen, in a conflict for English constitutional rights and privileges, and afterwards habituated (though in America) to keep an English people in a state of abject subjection, would prove fatal in the end to the liberties of England itself. (108)

They [Mr. Burke's detractors] quote his former speeches, and his former votes, but not one syllable from the book [*Reflections*]. It is only by a collation of the one with the other that the alledged inconsistency can be established. But as they are unable to cite any such contradictory passage, so neither can they shew any thing in the general tendency and spirit of the whole work unfavourable to a rational and generous spirit of liberty; unless a warm opposition to the spirit of levelling, to the spirit of impiety, to the spirit of proscription, plunder, murder, and cannibalism, be adverse to the true principles of freedom. (113)

The author [Burke] of that book [*Reflections*] is supposed to have passed from extreme to extreme; but he has always kept himself in a medium. This charge is not so wonderful. It is in the nature of things, that they who are in the centre of a circle should appear directly opposed to those who view them from any part of the circumference. (113)

The *purpose* for which the abuses of government are brought into view, forms a very material consideration in the mode of treating them. The complaints of a friend are things very different from the invectives of an enemy. (115)

He who, at the present time, is favourable, or even fair to that system [monarchy], must act towards it as towards a friend with frailties, who is under the prosecution of implacable foes. I think it a duty in that case, not to inflame the public mind against the obnoxious person, by any exaggeration of his faults. It is our duty rather to palliate his errors and defects, or to cast them into the shade, and industriously to bring forward any good qualities that he may happen to possess. But when the man is to be amended, and by amendment to be preserved, then the line of duty takes another direction. When his safety is effectually provided for, it then becomes the office of a friend to urge his faults and vices with all the energy of enlightened affection, to paint them in their most vivid colours, and to bring the moral patient to a better habit. Thus I think with regard to individuals; thus I think with regard to antient and respected governments and orders of men. A spirit of reforma-

tion is never more consistent with itself, than when it refuses to be
rendered the means of destruction. (115-116)

These new Whigs hold, that the sovereignty, whether exercised by
one or many, did not only originate from the people (a position not
denied, nor worth denying or assenting to) but that, in the people
the same sovereignty constantly and unalienably resides; that the
people may lawfully depose kings, not only for misconduct, but
without any misconduct at all; that they may set up any new fashion of government for themselves, or continue without any government at their pleasure; that the people are essentially their own
rule, and their will the measure of their conduct; that the tenure of
magistracy is not a proper subject of contract; because magistrates
have duties, but no rights: and that if a contract de facto is made
with them in one age, allowing that it binds at all, it only binds
those who were immediately concerned in it, but does not pass to
posterity. These doctrines concerning the people (a term which
they are far from accurately defining, but by which, from many circumstances, it is plain enough they mean their own faction, if they
should grow by early arming, by treachery, or violence, into the pre-
vailing force) tend, in my opinion, to the utter subversion, not only
of all government, in all modes, and to all stable securities to rational freedom, but to all the rules and principles of morality itself.

I assert, that the ancient Whigs held doctrines, totally different
from those I have last mentioned.

I now proceed to shew that the Whig managers for the Commons [the Old Whigs] meant to preserve the government on a firm
foundation, by asserting the perpetual validity of the settlement
then made, and its coercive power upon posterity. I mean to shew
that they gave no sort of countenance to any doctrine tending to

impress the people, taken separately from the legislature which includes the crown, with an idea that they had acquired a moral or civil competence to alter (without breach of the original compact on the part of the king) the succession to the crown, at their pleasure; much less that they had acquired any right, in the case of such an event as caused the Revolution, to set up any new form of government. (133)

Two things are equally evident, the first is, that the legislature possesses the power of regulating the succession of the crown, the second, that in the exercise of that right it has uniformly acted as if under the restraints which the author has stated. That author [Burke] makes what the antients call mos majorum [ancestral custom], not indeed his sole, but certainly his principal rule of policy, to guide his judgment in whatever regards our laws. Uniformity and analogy can be preserved in them by this process only. That point being fixed, and laying fast hold of a strong bottom, our speculations may swing in all directions, without public detriment; because they will ride with sure anchorage. (134-135)

These are the doctrines held by the Whigs of the Revolution [that is, the Old Whigs], delivered with as much solemnity, and as authentically at least, as any political dogmas were ever promulgated from the beginning of the world. If there be any difference between their tenets and those of Mr. Burke it is, that the old Whigs oppose themselves still more strongly than he does against the doctrines which are now propagated with so much industry by those who would be thought their successors. (146)

But it is his [Mr. Burke's] present concern, not to vindicate these old Whigs, but to shew his agreement with them. He appeals to them as judges: he does not vindicate them as culprits. It is current that these old politicians knew little of the rights of men; that they lost their way by groping about in the dark, and fumbling among rotten parchments and musty records. Great lights they say are lately obtained in the world; and Mr. Burke, instead of shrowding himself in exploded ignorance, ought to have taken advantage of the blaze of illumination which has been spread about him. It may be so. The enthusiasts of this time, it seems, like their predecessors in another faction of fanaticism, deal in lights . . .

The author of the Reflections has heard a great deal concerning the modern lights; but he has not yet had the good fortune to see much of them. He has read more than he can justify to any thing but the spirit of curiosity, of the works of these illuminators of the world. He has learned nothing from the far greater number of them, than a full certainty of their shallowness, levity, pride, petulance, presumption and ignorance . . . [I]t should seem they are the most likely to form the creed of the modern Whigs. (147-148)

Discuss any of their schemes—their answer is—It is the act of the people, and that is sufficient. Are we to deny to a majority of the people the right of altering even the whole frame of their society, if such should be their pleasure? They may change it, say they, from a monarchy to a republic to-day, and to-morrow back again from a republic to a monarchy; and so backward and forward as often as they like. They are masters of the commonwealth; because in substance they are themselves the commonwealth. The French revolution, say they, was the act of the majority of the people; and if the majority of any other people, the people of England for instance, wish to make the same change, they have the same right. (157)

The people are not to be taught to think lightly of their engagements to their governors; else they teach governors to think lightly
of their engagements towards them. In that kind of game in the end
the people are sure to be losers. To flatter them into a contempt of
faith, truth, and justice, is to ruin them; for in these virtues consists
their whole safety. To flatter any man, or any part of mankind, in
any description, by asserting, that in engagements he or they are
free whilst any other human creature is bound, is ultimately to vest
the rule of morality in the pleasure of those who ought to be rigidly
submitted to it; to subject the sovereign reason of the world to the
caprices of weak and giddy men. (158)

[M]en love to hear of their power, but have an extreme disrelish to
be told of their duty. This is of course; because every duty is a lim-
itation of some power. (158)

[A]rbitrary power is so much to the depraved taste of the vulgar,
of the vulgar of every description, that almost all the dissensions
which lacerate the commonwealth, are not concerning the manner
in which it is to be exercised, but concerning the hands in which
it is to be placed. (158)

It is not necessary to teach men to thirst after power. But it is very
expedient that, by moral instruction, they should be taught, and
by their civil constitutions they should be compelled, to put many
restrictions upon the immoderate exercise of it, and the inordinate
desire. (158)

The best method of obtaining these two great points [that is, the
putting of many restrictions upon the immoderate exercise of power and on the inordinate desire for power] forms the important, but

at the same time the difficult problem to the true statesman. He thinks of the place in which political power is to be lodged, with no other attention, than as it may render the more or the less practicable, its salutary restraint, and its prudent direction. For this reason no legislator, at any period of the world, has willingly placed the seat of active power in the hands of the multitude: Because there it admits of no control, no regulation, no steady direction whatsoever. The people are the natural control on authority; but to exercise and to control together is contradictory and impossible. (158-159)

Now though civil society might be at first a voluntary act (which in many cases it undoubtedly was) its continuance is under a permanent standing covenant, coexisting with the society; and it attaches upon every individual of that society, without any formal act of his own. This is warranted by the general practice, arising out of the general sense of mankind. Men without their choice derive benefits from that association; without their choice they are subjected to duties in consequence of these benefits; and without their choice they enter into a virtual obligation as binding as any that is actual. (159-160)

Look through the whole of life and the whole system of duties. Much the strongest moral obligations are such as were never the results of our option. (160)

We have obligations to mankind at large, which are not in consequence of any special voluntary pact. They arise from the relation of man to man, and the relation of man to God, which relations are not matters of choice. On the contrary, the force of all the pacts which we enter into with any particular person or number of persons amongst mankind, depends upon those prior obligations. In some cases the subordinate relations are voluntary, in others they are necessary—but the duties are all compulsive. When we marry, the choice is voluntary, but the duties are not matter of choice. They are dictated by the nature of the situation. Dark and inscrutable are the ways by which we come into the world. The instincts which give rise to this mysterious process of nature are not of our making. But out of physical causes, unknown to us, perhaps unknowable, arise moral duties, which, as we are able perfectly to comprehend, we are bound indispensably to perform. Parents may not be consenting to their moral relation; but consenting or not, they are bound to a long train of burthensome duties towards those with whom they have never made a convention of any sort. Children are not consenting to their relation, but their relation, without their actual consent, binds them to its duties; or rather it implies their consent because the presumed consent of every rational creature is in unison with the predisposed order of things. Men come in that manner into a community with the social state of their parents, endowed with all the benefits, loaded with all the duties of their situation. If the social ties and ligaments, spun out of those physical relations which are the elements of the commonwealth, in most cases begin, and always continue, independently of our will, so without any stipulation, on our part, are we bound by that relation called our country, which comprehends (as it has been well said) "all the charities of all" [Cicero]. Nor are we left without powerful instincts to make this duty as dear and grateful to us, as it is awful and coercive. Our country is not a thing of mere physical locality. It consists, in a great measure, in the antient order into which we are born. We may have the same geographical situation, but another country; as we may have the same country in another soil. The place that determines our duty to our country is a social, civil relation. (160-161)

I admit, indeed, that in morals, as in all things else, difficulties will sometimes occur. Duties will sometimes cross one another. Then questions will arise, which of them is to be placed in subordination; which of them may be entirely superseded? These doubts give rise to that part of moral science called casuistry; which, though necessary to be well studied by those who would become expert in that learning, who aim at becoming what, I think Cicero somewhere calls, artifices officiorum; it requires a very solid and discriminating judgment, great modesty and caution, and much sobriety of mind in the handling; else there is a danger that it may totally subvert those offices which it is its object only to methodize and reconcile. Duties, at their extreme bounds, are drawn very fine, so as to become almost evanescent. In that state, some shade of doubt will always rest on these questions, when they are pursued with great subtilty. But the very habit of stating these extreme cases is not very laudable or safe: because, in general, it is not right to turn our duties into doubts. They are imposed to govern our conduct, not to exercise our ingenuity; and therefore, our opinions about them ought not to be in a state of fluctuation, but steady, sure, and resolved. (162-163)

The practical consequences of any political tenet go a great way in deciding upon its value. Political problems do not primarily concern truth or falsehood. They relate to good or evil. What in the result is likely to produce evil, is politically false: that which is productive of good, politically true. (163)

We hear much from men, who have not acquired their hardiness of assertion from the profundity of their thinking, about the omnipotence of a majority, in such a dissolution of an ancient society as hath taken place in France. But amongst men so disbanded, there can be no such thing as majority or minority; or power in any one person to bind another. The power of acting by a majority, which the gentlemen theorists seem to assume so readily, after they have violated the contract out of which it has arisen (if at all it existed), must be grounded on two assumptions; first, that of an incorporation produced by unanimity; and secondly, an unanimous agreement, that the act of a mere majority (say of one) shall pass with them and with others as the act of the whole. (164)

[Here Burke speaks as though he were a Frenchman:]

Who are these insolent men calling themselves the French nation, that would monopolize this fair domain of nature? Is it because they speak a certain jargon? Is it their mode of chattering, to me unintelligible, that forms their title to my land? Who are they who claim by prescription and descent from certain gangs of banditti called Franks, and Burgundians, and Visigoths, of whom I may have never heard, and ninety-nine out of an hundred of themselves certainly never have heard; whilst at the very time they tell me, that prescription and long possession form no title to property? Who are they that presume to assert that the land which I purchased of the individual, a natural person, and not a fiction of state, belongs to them, who in the very capacity in which they make their claim can exist only as an imaginary being, and in virtue of the very prescription which they reject and disown? (166)

A true natural aristocracy is not a separate interest in the state, or separable from it. It is an essential integrant part of any large people rightly constituted. It is formed out of a class of legitimate presumptions, which, taken as generalities, must be admitted for actual truths. To be bred in a place of estimation; To see nothing low

and sordid from one's infancy; To be taught to respect one's self; To
be habituated to the censorial inspection of the public eye; To look
early to public opinion; To stand upon such elevated ground as to
be enabled to take a large view of the wide-spread and infinitely
diversified combinations of men and affairs in a large society; To
have leisure to read, to reflect, to converse; To be enabled to draw
the court and attention of the wise and learned wherever they are
to be found; To be habituated in armies to command and to obey;
To be taught to despise danger in the pursuit of honour and duty;
To be formed to the greatest degree of vigilance, foresight, and circumspection, in a state of things in which no fault is committed
with impunity, and the slightest mistakes draw on the most ruin-
ous consequences–To be led to a guarded and regulated conduct,
from a sense that you are considered as an instructor of your fel-
low-citizens in their highest concerns, and that you act as a recon-
ciler between God and man–To be employed as an administrator
of law and justice, and to be thereby amongst the first benefactors
to mankind–To be a professor of high science, or of liberal and
ingenuous art–To be amongst rich traders, who from their success
are presumed to have sharp and vigorous understandings, and to
possess the virtues of diligence, order, constancy, and regularity,
and to have cultivated an habitual regard to commutative justice–
These are the circumstances of men, that form what I should call
a natural aristocracy, without which there is no nation. (168)

[I]n all political questions the consequences of any assumed rights
are of great moment in deciding upon their validity. (175)

Get, say they, the possession of power by any means you can into
your hands; and then a subsequent consent (what they call an
address of adhesion) makes your authority as much the act of the

people as if they had conferred upon you originally that kind and degree of power, which, without their permission, you had seized upon. This is to give a direct sanction to fraud, hypocrisy, perjury, and the breach of the most sacred trusts that can exist between man and man .., This is to make the success of villainy the standard of innocence. (176-177)

[Burke says that many of the initial conveners in 1789 did not aim at revolution:]

When the several orders, in their several bailliages [bailiwicks, or jurisdictions], had met in the year 1789, such of them, I mean, as had met peaceably and constitutionally, to choose and to instruct their representatives, so organized, and so acting (because they were organized and were acting according to the conventions which made them a people), they were the people of France. They had a legal and a natural capacity to be considered as that people. But observe, whilst they were in this state, that is, whilst they were a people, in no one of their instructions did they charge or even hint at any of those things ... (177)

There are times and circumstances, in which not to speak out is at least to connive. Many think it enough for them, that the principles propagated by these clubs and societies enemies to their country and its constitution, are not owned by the modern Whigs in parliament, who are so warm in condemnation of Mr. Burke and his book [*Reflections*], and of course of all the principles of the ancient constitutional Whigs of this kingdom. Certainly they are not owned. But are they condemned with the same zeal as Mr. Burke and his book are condemned? Are they condemned at all? Are they rejected or discountenanced in any way whatsoever? (179)

But there is a wide difference between the multitude, when they act against their government from a sense of grievance, or from zeal for some opinions. When men are thoroughly possessed with that zeal, it is difficult to calculate its force. It is certain, that its power is by no means in exact proportion to its reasonableness. It must always have been discoverable by persons of reflection, but it is now obvious to the world, that a theory concerning government may become as much a cause of fanaticism as a dogma in religion. (182)

When a man is, from system, furious against monarchy or episco-pacy [church government], the good conduct of the monarch or the bishop has no other effect than further to irritate the adversary. He is provoked at it as furnishing a plea for preserving the thing which he wishes to destroy. His mind will be heated as much by the sight of a sceptre, a mace, or a verge [a rod used for punishment that came to symbolize authority], as if he had been daily bruised and wounded by these symbols of authority. Mere spectacles, mere names, will become sufficient causes to stimulate the people to war and tumult. (182)

Some gentlemen are not terrified by the facility with which govern-ment has been overturned in France. The people of France, they say, had nothing to lose in the destruction of a bad constitution; but though not the best possible, we have still a good stake in ours, which will hinder us from desperate risques. Is this any security at all against those who seem to persuade themselves, and who labour to persuade others, that our constitution is an usurpation in its ori-gin, unwise in its contrivance, mischievous in its effects, contrary to the rights of man, and in all its parts a perfect nuisance? (183)

In estimating danger, we are obliged to take into our calculation the character and disposition of the enemy into whose hands we may chance to fall. (185)

[R]iches do not in all cases secure even an inert and passive resistance. There are always, in that description, men whose fortunes, when their minds are once vitiated by passion or by evil principle, are by no means a security from their actually taking their part against the public tranquillity. We see to what low and despicable passions of all kinds many men in that class are ready to sacrifice the patrimonial estates, which might be perpetuated in their families with splendor, and with the fame of hereditary benefactors to mankind from generation to generation. Do we not see how lightly people treat their fortunes when under the influence of the passion of gaming [gambling]? The game of ambition or resentment will be played by many of the rich and great, as desperately, and with as much blindness to the consequences, as any other game. (191-192)

[I]f any thing bids fair for the prevention of so great a calamity, it must consist in the use of the ordinary means of just influence in society, whilst those means continue unimpaired. The public judgment ought to receive a proper direction. (192)

The moral sentiments, so nearly connected with early prejudice as to be almost one and the same thing, will assuredly not live long under a discipline, which has for its basis the destruction of all prejudices, and the making the mind proof against all dread of consequences flowing from the pretended truths that are taught by their philosophy. (193)

> [Burke's use of "prejudice" does not carry the negative connotations of the present. He means something like "prejudgments," "presumptions," or "priors."]

They who go with the principles of the ancient Whigs, which are those contained in Mr. Burke's book, never can go too far. They may indeed stop short of some hazardous and ambiguous excellence, which they will be taught to postpone to any reasonable degree of good they may actually possess. The opinions maintained in that book never can lead to an extreme, because their foundation is laid in an opposition to extremes. The foundation of government is there laid, not in imaginary rights of men (which at best is a confusion of judicial with civil principles), but in political convenience, and in human nature; either as that nature is universal, or as it is modified by local habits and social aptitudes. (193-194)

The whole scheme of our mixed constitution is to prevent any one of its principles from being carried as far, as taken by itself, and theoretically, it would go. Allow that to be the true policy of the British system, then most of the faults with which that system stands charged will appear to be, not imperfections into which it has inadvertently fallen, but excellencies which it has studiously sought. (194-195) He that sets his house on fire because his fingers are frostbitten, can never be a fit instructor in the method of providing our habitations with a cheerful and salutary warmth. (195-196)

This British constitution has not been struck out at an heat by a set of presumptuous men, like the assembly of pettifoggers [bad lawyers] run mad in Paris. . . . It is the result of the thoughts of many minds, in many ages. (196)

An ignorant man, who is not fool enough to meddle with his clock, is however sufficiently confident to think he can safely take to pieces, and put together at his pleasure, a moral machine of another guise, importance and complexity, composed of far other wheels, and springs, and balances, and counteracting and co-operating powers. Men little think how immorally they act in rashly meddling with what they do not understand. Their delusive good intention is no sort of excuse for their presumption. They who truly mean well must be fearful of acting ill. (196)

If we do not take to our aid the foregone studies of men reputed intelligent and learned, we shall be always beginners. (197)

But men must learn somewhere; and the new teachers mean no more than what they effect, as far as they succeed, that is, to deprive men of the benefit of the collected wisdom of mankind, and to make them blind disciples of their own particular presumption. (197)

Rational and experienced men, tolerably well know, and have always known, how to distinguish between true and false liberty. (198)

But none, except those who are profoundly studied, can comprehend the elaborate contrivance of a fabric fitted to unite private and public liberty with public force, with order, with peace, with justice, and, above all, with the institutions formed for bestowing permanence and stability through ages, upon this invaluable whole. (198)

Let us follow our ancestors, men not without a rational, though without an exclusive confidence in themselves; who, by respecting the reason of others, who, by looking backward as well as forward, by the modesty as well as by the energy of their minds, went on, insensibly drawing this constitution nearer and nearer to its perfection by never departing from its fundamental principles, nor introducing any amendment which had not a subsisting root in the laws, constitution, and usages of the kingdom. (199)

Thoughts on French Affairs
DECEMBER 1791

[The French Revolution] *is a Revolution of doctrine and theoretick dogma*. It has a much greater resemblance to those changes which have been made upon religious grounds, in which a spirit of proselytism makes an essential part. (208)

> [This is from a section where Burke argues the only event similar in scope and character to the French Revolution in European history was the Reformation.]

When I contemplate what [the French revolutionaries] have done at home, which is in effect little less than an amazing conquest wrought by a change of opinion, in a great part (to be sure far from altogether) very sudden, I cannot help letting my thoughts run along with their designs, and without attending to geographical order, to consider the other States of Europe so far as they may be any way affected by this astonishing Revolution. If early steps are not taken in some way or other to prevent the spreading of this influence, I scarcely think any of them perfectly secure. (221)

The world of contingency and political combination is much larger than we are apt to imagine. We never can say what may, or may not happen, without a view to all the actual circumstances. Experience upon other data than those, is of all things the most delusive. Prudence in new cases can do nothing on grounds of retrospect. A constant vigilance and attention to the train of things as they successively emerge, and to act on what they direct, are the only sure courses. (232)

It is not to be imagined because a political system is, under certain aspects, very unwise in its contrivance, and very mischievous in its effects, that it therefore can have no long duration. Its very defects may tend to its stability, because they are agreeable to its nature. (236)

[A]ll political measures depend on dispositions, tempers, means, and external circumstances, for all their effect . . . (254)

A Letter to Sir Hercules Langrishe on the Catholics of Ireland
JANUARY 1792

[T]imes and circumstances, considered with reference to the public, ought very much to govern our conduct; though I am far from slighting, when applied with discretion to those circumstances, general principles and maxims of policy. (197)

[The Popery laws, which were discriminated against Catholics] divided the nation [Ireland] into two distinct bodies, without common interest, sympathy or connexion; one of which bodies was to possess *all* the franchises, *all* the property, *all* the education: The others were to be drawers of water and cutters of turf for them. Are we to be astonished that when, by the efforts of so much violence in conquest, and so much policy in regulation, continued without intermission for near an hundred years, we had reduced them [Irish Catholics] to a mob; that whenever they came to act at all, many of them would act exactly like a mob, without temper, measure, or foresight? (198-199)

In the word *State,* I conceive there is much ambiguity. The state is sometimes used to signify *the whole common-wealth,* comprehending all its orders, with the several privileges belonging to each. Sometimes it signifies only *the higher and ruling part* of the common-wealth; which we commonly call *the Government.* In the first sense, to be under the state, but not the state itself, *nor any part of it,* is a situation perfectly intelligible: but to those who fill that situation, not very pleasant, when it is understood. It is a state of *civil servitude* by the very force of the definition.... In the other sense of the word *State,* by which is understood the *Supreme Government* only, I must observe this upon the question: that to exclude whole classes of men entirely from this *part* of government, cannot be considered as *absolute slavery.* It only implies a lower and degraded state of citizenship; such is (with more or less strictness) the condition of all countries, in which an hereditary nobility possess the exclusive rule. This may be no bad mode of government; provided that the personal authority of individual nobles be kept in due bounds, that their cabals and factions are guarded against with a severe vigilance: and that the people, (who have no share in granting their own money) are subjected to but light impositions, and are otherwise treated with attention, and with indulgence to their humours and prejudices. (200-201)

Our constitution is not made for great, general, and proscriptive exclusions; sooner or later, it will destroy them, or they will destroy the constitution. (204)

Lawful enjoyment is the surest method to prevent unlawful gratification. (207)

I am the most afraid of the weakest reasonings; because they discover the strongest passions. (228)

I believe no man will assert seriously, that when people are of a turbulent spirit, the best way to keep them in order, is to furnish them with something substantial to complain of. (229)

We must all obey the great law of change, it is the most powerful law of nature, and the means perhaps of its conservation. All we can do, and that human wisdom can do, is to provide that the change shall proceed by insensible degrees. (247)

Letter to William Elliot
MAY 1795

How often has public calamity been arrested on the very brink of ruin by the seasonable energy of a single man? Have we no such man amongst us? (272)

The great must submit to the dominion of prudence and of virtue; or none will long submit to the dominion of the great. (274)

A Letter to a Noble Lord
FEBRUARY 1796

I knew that there is a manifest marked distinction, which ill men, with ill designs, or weak men incapable of any design, will constantly be confounding, that is, a marked distinction between Change and Reformation. The former alters the substance of the objects themselves; and gets rid of all their essential good, as well as of all the accidental evil annexed to them. Change is novelty; and whether it is to operate any one of the effects of reformation at all, or whether it may not contradict the very principle upon which reformation is desired, cannot be certainly known beforehand. Reform is, not a change in the substance, or in the primary modification of the object, but a direct application of a remedy to the grievance complained of. So far as that is removed, all is sure. It stops there; and if it fails, the substance which underwent the operation, at the very worst, is but where it was. (290)

> [Burke builds upon this distinction between change and reformation throughout the letter.]

To innovate is not to reform. The French revolutionists complained of every thing; they refused to reform any thing; and they left nothing, no, nothing at all *unchanged.* (290-291)

A particular order of things may be altered; order itself cannot lose its value. As to other particulars, they are variable by time and by circumstances. Laws of regulation are not fundamental laws. The publick exigencies are the masters of all such laws. They rule the laws, and are not to be ruled by them. They who exercise the legislative power at the time must judge. (297)

[M]ere parsimony is not oeconomy. It is separable in theory from it; and in fact it may, or it may not, be a *part* of oeconomy, according to circumstances. Expence, and great expence, may be an essential part in true oeconomy. If parsimony were to be considered as one of the kinds of that virtue, there is however another and an higher oeconomy. Oeconomy is a distributive virtue, and consists not in saving, but in selection. Parsimony requires no providence, no sagacity, no powers of combination, no comparison, no judgment. Meer instinct, and that not an instinct of the noblest kind, may produce this false oeconomy in perfection. The other oeconomy has larger views. It demands a discriminating judgment, and a firm sagacious mind. (298)

> [By "oeconomy" here Burke means something like "frugality," not what we now call "the economy."]

It is a vile illiberal school, this new French academy of the sans culottes. (299)

> [The *sans-culottes* were commoners who supported the French Revolution. *Culottes* were fashionable pants worn by aristocrats.]

Ingratitude to benefactors is the first of revolutionary virtues. (311)

Nothing can be conceived more hard than the heart of a thorough-bred metaphysician. It comes nearer to the cold malignity of a wicked spirit than to the frailty and passion of a man. It is like that of the principle of Evil himself, incorporeal, pure, unmixed, dephlegmated, defecated evil. It is no easy operation to eradicate humanity from the human breast. (314-315)

[I]t is one fatal objection to all new fancied and new fabricated Republicks (among a people, who, once possessing such an advantage, have wickedly and insolently rejected it), that the prejudice of an old nobility is a thing that cannot be made. It may be improved, it may be corrected, it may be replenished: men may be taken from it, or aggregated to it, but the thing itself is matter of inveterate opinion, and therefore cannot be matter of mere positive institution... [T]his nobility, in fact does not exist in wrong of other orders of the state, but by them, and for them. (322)

Letters on a Regicide Peace
1795-96
Letter I

[C]ommonwealths are not physical but moral essences. They are artificial combinations; and, in their proximate efficient cause, the arbitrary productions of the human mind. We are not yet acquainted with the laws which necessarily influence the stability of that kind of work made by that kind of agent. There is not in the physical order ... a distinct cause by which any of those fabrics must necessarily grow, flourish, or decay; nor, in my opinion, does the moral world produce any thing more determinate on that subject, than what may serve as an amusement (liberal indeed, and ingenious, but still only an amusement) for speculative men. I doubt whether the history of mankind is yet complete enough, if ever it can be so, to furnish grounds for a sure theory on the internal causes which necessarily affect the fortune of a State. I am far from denying the operation of such causes: but they are infinitely uncertain, and much more obscure, and much more difficult to trace, than the foreign causes that tend to raise, to depress, and sometimes to overwhelm a community. (63)

We have seen States of considerable duration, which for ages
have remained nearly as they have begun, and could hardly be
said to ebb or flow. Some appear to have spent their vigour at
their commencement. Some have blazed out in their glory a little before their extinction. The meridian of some has been the
most splendid. Others, and they the greatest number, have fluc-
tuated, and experienced at different periods of their existence a
great variety of fortune. At the very moment when some of them
seemed plunged in unfathomable abysses of disgrace and disaster,
they have suddenly emerged. They have begun a new course, and
opened a new reckoning; and even in the depths of their calamity,
and on the very ruins of their country, have laid the foundations of
a towering and durable greatness. All this has happened without
any apparent previous change in the general circumstances which
had brought on their distress. The death of a man at a critical junc-
ture, his disgust, his retreat, his disgrace, have brought innumerable calamities on a whole nation. A common soldier, a child, a girl
at the door of an inn, have changed the face of fortune, and almost
of Nature. (63-64)

> [Burke makes a series of allusions in the last sentence, and we are
> indebted to the editors from Liberty Fund for explaining them.
> The "common soldier" is a reference to Arnold von Winkelried,
> who, according to legend, sacrificed himself in the 1386 Battle
> of Sempach and won a victory for Switzerland. The "child" is
> Hannibal, who swore an oath in his youth to forever be an ene-
> my of Rome. The "girl at the door of an inn" is Joan of Arc, who
> watched horses for an innkeeper before her famous acts.]

[T]he constitution of any political being, as well as that of any
physical being, ought to be known, before one can venture to say

what is fit for its conservation, or what is the proper means for its power. (66)

[I]t may be hoped, that through the medium of deliberate sober apprehension, we may arrive at steady fortitude. (66)

There is a courageous wisdom: there is also a false reptile prudence, the result not of caution but of fear. Under misfortunes it often happens that the nerves of the understanding are so relaxed, the pressing peril of the hour so completely confounds all the faculties, that no future danger can be properly provided for, can be justly estimated, can be so much as fully seen. The eye of the mind is dazzled and vanquished. An abject distrust of ourselves, an extravagant admiration of the enemy, present us with no hope but in a compromise with his pride, by a submission to his will. This short plan of policy is the only counsel which will obtain a hearing. We plunge into a dark gulph with all the rash precipitation of fear. The nature of courage is, without a question, to be conversant with danger; but in the palpable night of their terrors, men under consternation suppose, not that it is the danger, which, by a sure instinct, calls out the courage to resist it, but that it is the courage which produces the danger. They therefore seek for a refuge from their fears in the fears themselves, and consider a temporizing meanness as the only source of safety. (68-69)

The rules and definitions of prudence can rarely be exact; never universal. (69)

If wealth is the obedient and laborious slave of virtue and of publick honour, then wealth is in its place, and has its use. But if this order is changed, and honor is to be sacrificed to the conservation of riches, riches, which have neither eyes nor hands, nor any thing truly vital in them, cannot long survive the being of their vivifying powers, their legitimate masters, and their potent protectors. If we command our wealth, we shall be rich and free. If our wealth commands us, we are poor indeed. (69-70)

Often has a man lost his all because he would not submit to hazard all in defending it. (70)

A display of our wealth before robbers is not the way to restrain their boldness, or to lessen their rapacity. (70)

In a mass we cannot be left to ourselves. We must have leaders. If none will undertake to lead us right, we shall find guides who will contrive to conduct us to shame and ruin. (76)

There is a consanguinity between benevolence and humility. They are virtues of the same stock. (79)

A peace too eagerly sought, is not always the sooner obtained. The discovery of vehement wishes generally frustrates their attainment; and your adversary has gained a great advantage over you when he finds you impatient to conclude a treaty. There is in reserve, not only something of dignity, but a great deal of prudence too. A sort of courage belongs to negotiation, as well as to operations of the field. A negotiator must often seem willing to hazard the whole issue of his treaty, if he wishes to secure any one material point. (78)

The Regicides were the first to declare war. We are the first to sue for peace. (78)

It is the concern of mankind, that the destruction of order should not be a claim to rank: that crimes should not be the only title to preeminence and honour. (86)

I therefore wish to ask what hope we can have of their good faith, who, as the very basis of the negociation, assume the ill faith and treachery of those they have to deal with? (96)

Next they tell us, as a condition to our treaty, that "this Government must abjure the unjust hatred it bears to them, and at last open its ears to the voice of humanity." Truly this is even from them an extraordinary demand. Hitherto, it seems, we have put wax into our ears, to shut them up against the tender, soothing strains, in the *affettuoso* of humanity, warbled from the throats of Reubel, Carnot, Tallien, and the whole chorus of Confiscators, Domiciliary Visitors, Committee-men of Research, Jurors and Presidents of Revolutionary Tribunals, Regicides, Assassins, Massacrers, and Septembrizers. It is not difficult to discern what sort of humanity our Government is to learn from these syren singers. (99)

It is strange, but it may be true, that as the danger from Jacobinism is increased in my eyes and in yours, the fear of it is lessened in the eyes of many people who formerly regarded it with horror. It seems, they act under the impression of terrors of another sort, which have frightened them out of their first apprehensions. But let their fears, or their hopes, or their desires, be what they will, they should recollect, that they who would make peace without a previous knowledge of the terms, make a surrender. They are conquered. They do not treat; they receive the law. Is this the disposition of the people of England? Then the people of England ... are willing to trust to the sympathy of Regicides the guarantee of the

British Monarchy. They are content to rest their religion on the piety of atheists by establishment. They are satisfied to seek in the clemency of practised murderers the security of their lives. They are pleased to confide their property to the safeguard of those who are robbers by inclination, interest, habit, and system. (103-104)

In England and Scotland, I compute that those of adult age, not declining in life, of tolerable leisure for such discussions, and of some means of information, more or less, and who are above menial dependence, (or what virtually is such) may amount to about four hundred thousand. There is such a thing as a natural representative of the people. This body is that representative; and on this body, more than on the legal constituent, the artificial representative depends. (105)

[This is Burke's idea of "the public."]

Of these four hundred thousand political citizens, I look upon one fifth, or about eighty thousand, to be pure Jacobins; utterly incapable of amendment; objects of eternal vigilance; and when they break out, of legal constraint. On these, no reason, no argument, no example, no venerable authority, can have the slightest influence. They desire a change; and they will have it if they can. If they cannot have it by English cabal, they will make no sort of scruple of having it by the cabal of France, into which already they are virtually incorporated. (105)

These, by their spirit of intrigue, and by their restless agitating activity, are of a force far superior to their numbers; and if times grew the least critical, have the means of debauching or intimidating many of those who are now sound, as well as of adding to their force large bodies of the more passive part of the nation. This minority is numerous enough to make a mighty cry for peace, or for war, or for any object they are led vehemently to desire. By passing from place to place with a velocity incredible, and diversifying their character and description, they are capable of mimicking the general voice. We must not always judge of the generality of the opinion by the noise of the acclamation. (106)

All men that are ruined, are ruined on the side of their natural propensities. There they are unguarded. (106)

I have a good opinion of the general abilities of the Jacobins . . . [S]trong passions awaken the faculties. (107)

[T]he present [British] Ministry . . . must know that France is formidable not only as she is France, but as she is Jacobin France. They knew from the beginning that the Jacobin party was not confined to that country. They knew, they felt, the strong disposition of the same faction in both countries to communicate and to co-operate. For some time past, these two points have been kept, and even industriously kept, out of sight. France is considered as merely a foreign Power; and the seditious English only as a domestic faction. The merits of the war with the former have been argued solely on political grounds. To prevent the mischievous doctrines of the latter from corrupting our minds, matter and argument have been supplied abundantly, and even to surfeit, on the excellency of our own government. But nothing has been done to make us feel in what manner the safety of that Government is connected with the principle and with the issue of this war. For any thing which in the late discussion has appeared, the war is entirely collateral to the state of Jacobinism; as truly a foreign war to us and to all our home concerns, as the war with Spain in 1739, about *Guarda-Costas*, the Madrid Convention, and the fable of Captain Jenkins's ears. (110)

> [Burke is referring to the War of Jenkins' Ear, which lasted from 1739-1748 and was fought between Britain and Spain. A British sailor named Jenkins lost his ear in a fight with Spanish sailors, and supposedly the ear was shown in Parliament to rally support for the war. The *Guarda-Costas* were the Spanish coast guard in North America. The Madrid Convention was a 1713 agreement that gave Britain a monopoly on supplying slaves for Spanish colonies.]

[War] is never to be entered into without a mature deliberation; not a deliberation lengthened out into a perplexing indecision, but a deliberation leading to a sure and fixed judgment. When so taken up, it is not to be abandoned without reason as valid, as fully and as extensively considered. Peace may be made as unadvisedly as war. Nothing is so rash as fear; and the counsels of pusillanimity very rarely put off, whilst they are always sure to aggravate, the evils from which they would fly. (120)

In that great war carried on against Louis the Fourteenth, for near eighteen years, Government spared no pains to satisfy the nation that, though they were to be animated by a desire of glory, glory was not their ultimate object; but that every thing dear to them, in religion, in law, in liberty—every thing which as freemen, as Englishmen, and as citizens of the great commonwealth of Christendom, they had at heart, was then at stake. (120-121)

> [Burke is referring to the War of the Spanish Succession (1701-1714) and other hostilities.]

If to preserve political independence and civil freedom to nations, was a just ground of war; a war to preserve national independence, property, liberty, life, and honour, from certain universal havock, is a war just, necessary, manly, pious; and we are bound to persevere in it by every principle, divine and human, as long as the system which menaces them all, and all equally, has an existence in the world. (122)

France, since her Revolution, is under the sway of a sect, whose leaders have deliberately, at one stroke, demolished the whole body of that jurisprudence which France had pretty nearly in common with other civilized countries. In that jurisprudence were contained the elements and principles of the law of nations, the great ligament of mankind. With the law they have of course destroyed all seminaries in which jurisprudence was taught, as well as all the corporations established for it's conservation. I have not heard of any country, whether in Europe or Asia, or even in Africa on this side of Mount Atlas [the Atlas Mountains], which is wholly without some such colleges and such corporations, except France. No man, in a publick or private concern, can divine by what rule or principle her judgments are to be directed; nor is there to be found a professor in any University, or a practitioner in any Court, who will hazard an opinion of what is or is not law in France, in any case whatever. (123-124)

Instead of the religion and the law by which they were in a great politick communion with the Christian world, [the Jacobins] have constructed their Republick on three bases, all fundamentally opposite to those on which the communities of Europe are built. Its foundation is laid in Regicide; in Jacobinism; and in Atheism;

and it has joined to those principles, a body of systematick manners which secures their operation. (124)

I call a commonwealth Regicide, which lays it down as a fixed law of nature, and a fundamental right of man, that all government, not being a democracy, is an usurpation; that all Kings, as such, are usurpers, and for being Kings, may and ought to be put to death, with their wives, families, and adherents. The commonwealth which acts uniformly upon those principles; and which after abolishing every festival of religion, chooses the most flagrant act of a murderous Regicide treason for a feast of eternal commemoration, and which forces all her people to observe it—this I call Regicide by establishment. (124-125)

Jacobinism is the revolt of the enterprising talents of a country against its property. When private men form themselves into associations for the purpose of destroying the pre-existing laws and institutions of their country; when they secure to themselves an army by dividing amongst the people of no property, the estates of the ancient and lawful proprietors; when a state recognizes those acts; when it does not make confiscations for crimes, but makes crimes for confiscations; when it has its principal strength, and all its resources in such a violation of property; when it stands chiefly upon such a violation; massacring by judgments, or otherwise, those who make any struggle for their old legal government, and their legal, hereditary, or acquired possessions—I call this *Jacobinism by Establishment*. (125)

Manners are of more importance than laws. Upon them, in a great measure, the laws depend. The law touches us but here and there, and now and then. Manners are what vex or sooth, corrupt or purify, exalt or debase, barbarize or refine us, by a constant, steady, uniform, insensible operation, like that of the air we breathe in. They give their whole form and colour to our lives. According to their quality, they aid morals, they supply them, or they totally destroy them. (126)

The whole drift of [the Jacobins'] institution is contrary to that of the wise Legislators of all countries, who aimed at improving instincts into morals, and at grafting the virtues on the stock of the natural affections. They, on the contrary, have omitted no pains to eradicate every benevolent and noble propensity in the mind of men. In their culture it is a rule always to graft virtues on vices. They think everything unworthy of the name of publick virtue, unless it indicates violence on the private. All their new institutions, (and with them every thing is new,) strike at the root of our social nature. Other Legislators, knowing that marriage is the origin of all relations, and consequently the first element of all duties, have endeavoured, by every art, to make it sacred. The Christian Religion, by confining it to the pairs, and by rendering that relation indissoluble, has, by these two things, done more towards the peace, happiness, settlement, and civilization of the world, than by any other part in this whole scheme of Divine Wisdom. (127)

There have been periods of time in which communities, apparently in peace with each other, have been more perfectly separated than, in later times, many nations in Europe have been in the course of long and bloody wars. The cause must be sought in the similitude throughout Europe of religion, laws, and manners. At bottom, these are all the same. The writers on public law have often called this aggregate of nations a Commonwealth. They had reason. It is virtually one great state having the same basis of general law; with some diversity of provincial customs and local establishments. The nations of Europe have had the very same christian religion, agreeing in the fundamental parts, varying a little in the ceremonies and in the subordinate doctrines. The whole of the polity and oeconomy of every country in Europe has been derived from the same sources. It was drawn from the old Germanic or Gothic custumary; from the feudal institutions which must be considered as an emanation from that custumary; and the whole has been improved and digested into system and discipline by the Roman law. From hence arose the several orders, with or without a Monarch, which are called States, in every European country; the strong traces of which, where Monarchy predominated, were never wholly extinguished or merged in despotism. In the few places where Monarchy was cast off, the spirit of European Monarchy was still left. Those countries still continued countries of States; that is, of classes, orders, and distinctions, such as had before subsisted, or nearly so. Indeed the force and form of the institution called States, continued in greater perfection in those republican communities than under Monarchies. From all those sources arose a system of manners and of education which was nearly similar in all this quarter of the globe; and which softened, blended, and harmonized the colours of the whole. There was little difference in the form of the Universities for the education of their youth, whether with regard to faculties, to sciences, or to the more liberal and elegant kinds of erudition. From this resemblance in the modes of intercourse, and in the whole form and fashion of life, no citizen of Europe could be altogether an exile in any part of it. There was nothing more than a pleasing variety to recreate and instruct the mind, to enrich the imagination, and to meliorate the heart. When a man travelled or resided for health, pleasure, business or necessity, from his own country, he never felt himself quite abroad. (133-134)

[Burke is surely overstating the similarities between European countries. It seems his purpose in doing so is to emphasize the commonalities between European countries and characterize Jacobinism as an outside threat to that order. One might consider this a forerunner to modern talk of "the free world."]

I defy the most refining ingenuity to invent any other cause for the total departure of the Jacobin Republick from every one of the ideas and usages, religious, legal, moral, or social, of this civilized world, and for her tearing herself from its communion with such studied violence, but from a formed resolution of keeping no terms with that world. It has not been, as has been falsely and insidiously represented, that these miscreants had only broke with their old Government. (134)

This violent breach of the community of Europe we must conclude to have been made, (even if they had not expressly declared it over and over again) [forcing mankind] either . . . into an adoption of their system, or to live in perpetual enmity with a community the most potent we have ever known. (134-135)

[T]here is a sort of presumption against novelty, drawn out of a deep consideration of human nature and human affairs; and the maxim of jurisprudence is well laid down, *Vetustas pro lege semper habetur* [Ancient custom is always held as law]. (136)

The State, in its essence, must be moral and just: and it may be so, though a tyrant or usurper should be accidentally at the head of it. This is a thing to be lamented: but this notwithstanding, the body of the commonwealth may remain in all its integrity and be perfectly sound in its composition. The present case is different. It is not a revolution in government. It is not the victory of party over party. It is a destruction and decomposition of the whole society; which never can be made of right by any faction, however powerful, nor without terrible consequences to all about it, both in the act and in the example. This pretended Republick is founded in crimes, and exists by wrong and robbery; and wrong and robbery, far from a title to any thing, is war with mankind. To be at peace with robbery is to be an accomplice with it. (139)

Nation is a moral essence, not a geographical arrangement, or a denomination of the nomenclator. (139)

Example is the school of mankind, and they will learn at no other. (143)

When it appears evident to our governors that our desires and our interests are at variance, they ought not to gratify the former at the expence of the latter. Statesmen are placed on an eminence, that they may have a larger horizon than we can possibly command. They have a whole before them, which we can contemplate only in the parts, and even without the necessary relations. Ministers are not only our natural rulers but our natural guides. Reason, clearly and manfully delivered, has in itself a mighty force: but reason in the mouth of legal authority, is, I may fairly say, irresistible.

I admit that reason of state will not, in many circumstances, permit the disclosure of the true ground of a public proceeding. In that case, silence is manly; and it is wise. It is fair to call for trust when the principle of reason itself suspends its public use. I take the distinction to be this. The ground of a particular measure, making a part of a plan, it is rarely proper to divulge. All the broader grounds of policy on which the general plan is to be adopted, ought as rarely to be concealed. They who have not the whole cause before them, call them politicians, call them people, call them what you will, are no judges. The difficulties of the case, as well as its fair side, ought to be presented. This ought to be done: and it is all that can be done. When we have our true situation distinctly presented to us, if then we resolve, with a blind and headlong violence, to resist the admonitions of our friends, and to cast ourselves into the hands of our potent and irreconcileable foes, then, and not till then, the ministers stand acquitted before God and man, for whatever may come. (147-148)

I do not forget that there had been a considerable difference between several of our friends, with my insignificant self, and the great man [William Pitt] at the head of Ministry, in an early stage of these discussions. But I am sure there was a period in which we agreed better in the danger of a Jacobin existence in France. At one time, he and all Europe seemed to feel it. But why am not I converted with so many great Powers, and so many great Ministers? It is because I am old and slow. I am in this year, 1796, only where all the powers of Europe were in 1793. (150-1)

In this crisis I must hold my tongue, or I must speak with freedom. Falsehood and delusion are allowed in no case whatever: but, as in the exercise of all the virtues, there is an oeconomy of truth. It is a sort of temperance, by which a man speaks truth with measure that he may speak it the longer. But, as the same rules do not hold in all cases, what would be right for you, who may presume on a series of years before you, would have no sense for me, who cannot, without absurdity, calculate on six months of life. What I say, I must say at once. Whatever I write is in its nature testamentary. It may have the weakness, but it has the sincerity of a dying declaration. For the few days I have to linger here, I am removed completely from the busy scene of the world; but I hold myself to be still responsible for every thing that I have done whilst I continued on the place of action. If the rawest tyro [newcomer] in politicks has been influenced by the authority of my grey hairs, and led by any thing in my speeches, or my writings, to enter into this war, he has a right to call upon me to know why I have changed my opinions, or why, when those I voted with, have adopted better notions, I persevere in exploded errour.

When I seem not to acquiesce in the acts of those I respect in every degree short of superstition, I am obliged to give my reasons fully. (151)

Letter II, on a Regicide Peace

I conceived that the contest [with France], once begun, could not be laid down again to be resumed at our discretion; but that our first struggle with this evil would also be our last. I never thought we could make peace with the [French revolutionary] system; because it was not for the sake of an object we pursued in rivalry with each other, but with the system itself, that we were at war. As I understood the matter, we were at war, not with its conduct, but with its existence; convinced that its existence and its hostility were the same. (155)

The faction is not local or territorial. It is a general evil. Where it least appears in action, it is still full of life. In its sleep it recruits its strength, and prepares its exertion. Its spirit lies deep in the corruptions of our common nature. The social order which restrains it, feeds it. It exists in every country in Europe; and among all orders of men in every country, who look up to France as to a common head. The centre is there. The circumference is the world of Europe wherever the race of Europe may be settled. Everywhere else the faction is militant; in France it is triumphant. In France is the bank of deposit, and the bank of circulation, of all the pernicious principles that are forming in every State. It will be a folly scarcely deserving of pity, and too mischievous for contempt, to think of restraining it in any other country whilst it is predominant there. (155)

[I]n ability, in dexterity, in the distinctness of their views, the Jacobins are our superiors. They saw the thing right from the very beginning. Whatever were the first motives to the war among politicians, they saw that it is in its spirit, and for its objects, a *civil war*; and as such they pursued it. It is a war between the partizans of the ancient, civil, moral, and political order of Europe against a sect of fanatical and ambitious atheists which means to change them all. It is not France extending a foreign empire over other nations: it is a sect aiming at universal empire, and beginning with the conquest of France. The leaders of that sect secured the *centre of Europe*; and that secured, they knew, that whatever might be the event of battles and sieges, their cause was victorious. Whether its territory had a little more or a little less peeled from its surface, or whether an island or two was detached from its commerce, to them was of little moment. The conquest of France was a glorious acquisition. That once well laid as a basis of empire, opportunities never could be wanting to regain or to replace what had been lost, and dreadfully to avenge themselves on the faction of their adversaries.

They saw it was a civil war. It was their business to persuade their adversaries that it ought to be a foreign war. (157)

If armies and fortresses were a defence against Jacobinism, Louis the Sixteenth would this day reign a powerful monarch over an happy people. (159)

> [Louis XVI (1754-1793) was the King of France when the revolution took place. The French army did indeed have many fortresses, but they did not stop the revolutionaries from beheading Louis by guillotine.]

We shall reflect at leisure on one great truth, that it was ten times more easy totally to destroy the system itself, than when established, it would be to reduce its power: and that this Republick [the Regicide system], most formidable abroad, was, of all things, the weakest at home. That her frontier was terrible, her interior feeble; that it was matter of choice to attack her where she is invincible, and to spare her where she was ready to dissolve by her own internal disorders. We shall reflect, that our plan was good neither for offence nor defence. (164)

It would not be at all difficult to prove that an army of a hundred thousand men, horse, foot, and artillery, might have been employed against the enemy on the very soil which he has usurped, at a far less expense than has been squandered away upon tropical adventures . . . Had we carried on the war on the side of France which looks towards the Channel or the Atlantick, we should have attacked our enemy on his weak and unarmed side. We should not have to reckon on the loss of a man, who did not fall in battle. We should have an ally in the heart of the country, who to our hundred thousand, would at one time have added eighty thousand men at the least, and all animated by principle, by enthusiasm, and by vengeance: motives which secured them to the cause in a very different manner from some of our allies whom we subsidized with millions.

This ally, or rather this principal in the war, by the confession of the Regicide himself, was more formidable to him than all his other foes united. Warring there, we should have led our arms to the capital of Wrong. Defeated, we could not fail (proper precautions taken) of a sure retreat. Stationary, and only supporting the Royalists, an impenetrable barrier, an impregnable rampart, would have been formed between the enemy and his naval power. We are probably the only nation who have declined to act against an enemy, when it might have been done in his own country; and who having an armed, a powerful, and a long victorious ally in that country, declined all effectual cooperation, and suffered him to perish for want of support. On the plan of a war in France, every advantage that our allies might gain would be doubled in its effect. Disasters on the one side might have a fair chance of being compensated by victories on the other. Had we brought the main of our force to bear upon that quarter, all the operations of the British and Imperial crowns would have been combined. The war would have had system, correspondence, and a certain direction. But as the war has been pursued, the operations of the two crowns have not the smallest degree of mutual bearing or relation. (164-165)

Unfortunately . . . a war in a wholesome climate, a war at our door, a war directly on the enemy, a war in the heart of his country, a war in concert with an internal ally, and in combination with the external, is regarded as folly and romance. (167)

The social nature of man impels him to propagate his principles, as much as physical impulses urge him to propagate his kind. The passions give zeal and vehemence. The understanding bestows design and system. The whole man moves under the discipline of his opinions. Religion is among the most powerful causes of enthusiasm. When any thing concerning it becomes an object of much meditation, it cannot be indifferent to the mind. They who do not love religion, hate it. ... They cannot strike the Sun out of Heaven, but they are able to raise a smouldering smoke that obscures him from their own eyes. Not being able to revenge themselves on God, they have a delight in vicariously defacing, degrading, torturing, and tearing in pieces his image in man. Let no one judge of them by what he has conceived of them, when they were not incorporated, and had no lead. ... But when the possibility of dominion, lead, and propagation presented themselves, and that the ambition, which before had so often made them hypocrites, might rather gain than lose by a daring avowal of their sentiments, then the nature of this infernal spirit, which has 'evil for its good,' [a reference to *Paradise Lost*] appeared in its full perfection. Nothing, indeed, but the possession of some power, can with any certainty discover what at the bottom is the true character of any man. Without reading the speeches of Vergniaux, Français of Nantz, Isnard, and some others of that sort, it would not be easy to conceive the passion, rancour, and malice of their tongues and hearts. (170-171)

[Burke lists three Girondist politicians from the Revolution. The Girondists were Jacobins, but they differed from the more radical Montagnards. When the Montagnards, led by Robespierre, took power, they purged the Girondists in the Reign of Terror. Pierre Victurnien Vergniaud (1753-1793), which Burke spells "Vergniaux," was a leader in the Girondist faction during the Revolution known for his speaking abilities. As his year of death portends, he was executed during the Reign of Terror. Français of Nantes (1756-1836) was a French noble. He fled during the Reign of Terror and returned when it was safe, remaining active in the politics of the First Empire. Maximin Isnard (1755-1825) was president of the National Convention before the Reign of Terror began. He fled and returned to serve

again in the post-Terror government. Burke seems to be indi-
cating that even these more moderate Jacobins, who fell victim
to the radical Jacobins, were still too radical for comfort.]

Nothing, indeed, but the possession of some power, can with any
certainty discover what at the bottom is the true character of any
man. (171)

The unfortunate Louis the Sixteenth was not the first cause of the
evil by which he suffered. He came to it, as to a sort of inheritance,
by the false politicks of his immediate predecessor. This system of
dark and perplexed intrigue had come to its perfection before he
came to the throne: and even then the Revolution strongly oper-
ated in all its causes. (174)

The States of the Christian World have grown up to their present
magnitude in a great length of time, and by a great variety of acci-
dents. They have been improved to what we see them with greater or less degrees of felicity and skill. Not one of them has been
formed upon a regular plan or with any unity of design. As their
Constitutions are not systematical, they have not been directed to
any *peculiar* end, eminently distinguished, and superseding every
other. The objects which they embrace are of the greatest possible variety, and have become in a manner infinite. In all these old
countries the state has been made to the people, and not the people conformed to the state. Every state has pursued, not only every
sort of social advantage, but it has cultivated the welfare of every
individual. His wants, his wishes, even his tastes have been con-
sulted. This comprehensive scheme virtually produced a degree
of personal liberty in forms the most adverse to it. That liberty
was found, under monarchies stiled absolute, in a degree unknown

to the ancient commonwealths. From hence the powers of all our modern states meet in all their movements with some obstruction. It is therefore no wonder, that when these states are to be considered as machines to operate for some one great end, that this dissipated and balanced force is not easily concentered, or made to bear with the whole nation upon one point. (180-181)

The British State is, without question, that which pursues the greatest variety of ends, and is the least disposed to sacrifice any one of them to another, or to the whole. It aims at taking in the entire circle of human desires, and securing for them their fair enjoyment. Our legislature has been ever closely connected, in its most efficient part, with individual feeling and individual interest. Personal liberty, the most lively of these feelings and the most important of these interests, which in other European countries has rather arisen from the system of manners and the habitudes of life, than from the laws of the state, (in which it flourished more from neglect than attention) in England has been a direct object of Government. (181)

What now stands as Government in France is struck out at a heat. The design is wicked, immoral, impious, oppressive; but it is spirited and daring: it is systematick; it is simple in its principle; it has unity and consistency in perfection. In that country entirely to cut off a branch of commerce, to extinguish a manufacture, to destroy the circulation of money, to violate credit, to suspend the course of agriculture, even to burn a city, or to lay waste a province of their own, does not cost them a moment's anxiety. To them, the will, the wish, the want, the liberty, the toil, the blood of individuals is as nothing. Individuality is left out of their scheme of Government. The state is all in all. Every thing is referred to the production of force; afterwards every thing is trusted to the use of it.

It is military in its principle, in its maxims, in its spirit, and in all its movements. The state has dominion and conquest for its sole objects; dominion over minds by proselytism, over bodies by arms.

Thus constituted with an immense body of natural means, which are lessened in their amount only to be increased in their effect, France has, since the accomplishment of the Revolution, a complete unity in its direction. It has destroyed every resource of the State which depends upon opinion and the good-will of individuals. The riches of convention disappear. (182)

We go about asking when *assignats* will expire, and we laugh at the last price of them. But what signifies the fate of those tickets of despotism? The despotism will find despotick means of supply. They have found the short cut to the productions of Nature, while others, in pursuit of them, are obliged to wind through the labyrinth of a very intricate state of society. They seize upon the fruit of the labour; they seize upon the labourer himself. (182)

> [*Assignats* were paper money issued by the revolutionary government. They were backed by the value of stolen church property and notorious for hyperinflation.]

Ought we to judge from the excise and stamp duties of the rocks, or from the paper circulation of the sands of Arabia, the power by which Mahomet [Muhammad] and his tribes laid hold at once on the two most powerful Empires of the world; beat one of them totally to the ground, broke to pieces the other, and, in not much longer space of time than I have lived, overturned governments, laws, manners, religion, and extended an empire from the Indus to the Pyrenees?

Material resources never have supplied, nor ever can supply, the want of unity in design and constancy in pursuit.(183)

> [Burke gives the example of the spread of Islam and its political
> effects to illustrate how ideas are more important than natural
> resources in determining the course of events.]

Reflect, my dear Sir, reflect again and again on a Government, in
which the property is in complete subjection, and where nothing
rules but the mind of desperate men.... [I]f the world will shut their
eyes to this state of things, they will feel it more. (183)

The correspondence of the monied and the mercantile world, the
literary intercourse of academies, but, above all, the press, of which
they had in a manner, entire possession, made a kind of electrick
communication every where. The press, in reality, has made every
Government, in its spirit, almost democratick. (186)

Letter III, on a Regicide Peace

Virtues have their place; and out of their place they hardly deserve
the name. They pass into the neighbouring vice. The patience of
fortitude, and the endurance of pusillanimity, are things very different, as in their principle, so in their effects. (203)

Men are rarely without some sympathy in the sufferings of others; but in the immense and diversified mass of human misery,
which may be pitied, but cannot be relieved, in the gross, the
mind must make a choice. Our sympathy is always more forcibly
attracted towards the misfortunes of certain persons, and in certain

descriptions: and this sympathetic attraction discovers, beyond a possibility of mistake, our mental affinities, and elective affections. It is a much surer proof, than the strongest declaration, of a real connexion and of an over-ruling bias in the mind. (210)

Strong passion under the direction of a feeble reason feeds a low fever, which serves only to destroy the body that entertains it. But vehement passion does not always indicate an infirm judgment. It often accompanies, and actuates, and is even auxiliary to a powerful understanding; and when they both conspire and act harmoniously, their force is great to destroy disorder within, and to repel injury from abroad. (218)

Fraud and prevarication are servile vices. They sometimes grow out of the necessities, always out of the habits of slavish and degenerate spirits: and on the theatre of the world, it is not by assuming the mask of a Davus or a Geta [characters in a Roman play] that an actor will obtain credit for manly simplicity and a liberal openness of proceeding. It is an erect countenance: it is a firm adherence to principle; it is a power of resisting false shame and frivolous fear, that assert our good faith and honour, and assure to us the confidence of mankind. (224)

I positively assert, that the people have no where, and in no way, expressed their wish of throwing themselves and their Sovereign at the feet of a wicked and rancorous foe . . . It is undoubtedly the business of Ministers very much to consult the inclinations of the people, but they ought to take great care that they do not receive that inclination from the few persons who may happen to approach them. The petty interests of such gentlemen, their low conceptions of things, their fears arising from the danger to which the very

arduous and critical situation of publick affairs may expose their
places; their apprehensions from the hazards to which the discon-
tents of a few popular men at elections may expose their seats in
Parliament–all these causes trouble and confuse the representa-
tions which they make to Ministers of the real temper of the nation.
If Ministers, instead of following the great indications of the Constitution, proceed on such reports, they will take the whispers of
a cabal for the voice of the people, and the counsels of imprudent
timidity for the wisdom of a nation. (237-238)

Exploding, therefore, all sorts of balances, they [the current French
rulers] avow their design to erect themselves into a new description
of Empire, which is not grounded on any balance, but forms a sort
of impious hierarchy, of which France is to be the head and the
guardian. The law of this their Empire is any thing rather than
the publick law of Europe, the antient conventions of its several
States ... They permit, and that is all, the temporary existence of
some of the old communities; but whilst they give to these tolerated States this temporary respite in order to secure them in a condition of real dependence on themselves, they invest them on every
side by a body of Republicks, formed on the model, and dependent
ostensibly, as well as substantially, on the will, of the mother Republick to which they owe their origin. These are to be so many gar-
risons to check and controul the States which are to be permitted
to remain on the old model, until they are ripe for a change. It is in
this manner that France, on her new system, means to form an universal empire, by producing an universal revolution. By this means,
forming a new code of communities according to what she calls the
natural rights of man and of States, she pretends to secure eternal
peace to the world, guaranteed by her generosity and justice, which
are to grow with the extent of her power. To talk of the balance

of power to the governors of such a country, was a jargon which they could not understand even through an interpreter. (247-248)

Before men can transact any affair, they must have a common language to speak, and some common recognised principles on which they can argue. Otherwise, all is cross-purpose and confusion. (248)

But ... we still flatter ourselves that the publick voice of France will compel this Directory to more moderation. Whence does this hope arise? What publick voice is there in France? There are, indeed, some writers, who, since this monster of a Directory has obtained a great regular military force to guard them, are indulged in a sufficient liberty of writing, and some of them write well undoubtedly. But the world knows that in France there is no publick, that the country is composed but of two descriptions; audacious tyrants and trembling slaves. The contest between the tyrants is the only vital principle that can be discerned in France. The only thing which there appears like spirit, is amongst the late associates, and fastest friends of the Directory, the more furious and untameable part of the Jacobins. This discontented member of the faction does almost balance the reigning divisions; and it threatens every moment to predominate. For the present, however, the dread of their fury forms some sort of security to their fellows, who now exercise a more regular, and therefore a somewhat less ferocious tyranny. Most of the slaves chuse a quiet, however reluctant, submission to those who are somewhat satiated with blood, and who, like wolves, are a little more tame from being a little less hungry, in preference to an irruption of the famished devourers who are prowling and howling about the fold. (253)

[The Directory was France's form of government from 1795-1799, after the Reign of Terror and before Napoleon's First Empire.]

Necessity, as it has no law, so it has no shame; but moral necessity is not like metaphysical, or even physical. In that category, it is a word of loose signification, and conveys different ideas to different minds. To the low-minded, the slightest necessity becomes an invincible necessity. . . .But when the necessity pleaded is not in the nature of things, but in the vices of him who alleges it, the whining tones of common-place beggarly rhetorick produce nothing but indignation; because they indicate a desire of keeping up a dishonourable existence, without utility to others, and without dignity to itself; because they aim at obtaining the dues of labour without industry; and by frauds would draw from the compassion of others, what men ought to owe to their own spirit and their own exertions. (254)

The moment a man is exempted from the maintenance of the community, he is in a sort separated from it. He loses the place of a citizen. (257)

There must be some impulse besides public spirit, to put private interest into motion along with it. Monied men ought to be allowed to set a value on their money; if they did not, there could be no monied men. This desire of accumulation is a principle without which the means of their service to the State could not exist. The love of lucre, though sometimes carried to a ridiculous, sometimes to a vicious excess, is the grand cause of prosperity to all States. In this natural, this reasonable, this powerful, this prolifick principle, it is for the satyrist to expose the ridiculous; it is for the moralist to censure the vicious; it is for the sympathetick heart to reprobate the hard and cruel; it is for the Judge to animadvert on the fraud, the extortion, and the oppression: but it is for the Statesman to employ it as he finds it, with all its concomitant excellencies, with all its imperfections on its head. It is his part, in this case, as it is in all other cases, where he is to make use of the general energies of nature, to take them as he finds them. (258)

After all, it is a great mistake to imagine, as too commonly, almost indeed generally, it is imagined, that the publick borrower and the private lender are two adverse parties with different and contending interests, and that what is given to the one, is wholly taken from the other. Constituted as our system of finance and taxation is, the interests of the contracting parties cannot well be separated, whatever they may reciprocally intend. (258)

Let Government protect and encourage industry, secure property, repress violence, and discountenance fraud, it is all that they have to do. In other respects, the less they meddle in these affairs the better; the rest is in the hands of our Master and theirs. (267)

I do not call a healthy young man, chearful in his mind, and vigorous in his arms—I cannot call such a man, poor; I cannot pity my kind as a kind, merely because they are men. This affected pity only tends to dissatisfy them with their condition, and to teach them to seek resources where no resources are to be found—in something else than their own industry, and frugality, and sobriety. (268)

Our physical well-being, our moral worth, our social happiness, our political tranquillity, all depend on that controul of all our appetites and passions, which the ancients designed by the cardinal virtue of Temperance. (273)

[I]f in our own history, there is any one circumstance to which, under God, are to be attributed the steady resistance, the fortunate issue, and sober settlement, of all our struggles for liberty, it is, that while the landed interest, instead of forming a separate body, as in other countries, has, at all times, been in close connexion and union with the other great interests of the country, it has been spontaneously allowed to lead and direct, and moderate all the rest. (292)

Letter IV, on a Regicide Peace

These ephemerides of politicks are not made for our slow and coarse understandings. Our appetite demands a piece of resistance. We require some food that will stick to the ribs. We call for sentiments, to which we can attach ourselves; sentiments, in which we can take an interest; sentiments, on which we can warm, on which we can ground some confidence in ourselves or in others. (313)

> [With "ephemerides of politicks" Burke likens decrees and actions in France to comets or meteors, whose appearance is ephemeral.]

Five years has this Monster [the Revolution] continued whole and entire in all its members. Far from falling into a division within itself, it is augmented by tremendous additions. We cannot bear to look that frightful form in the face as it is and in its own actual shape. We dare not be wise. We have not the fortitude of rational fear. We will not provide for our future safety; but we endeavour to hush the cries of present timidity by guesses at what may be hereafter. "To-morrow, and to-morrow, and to-morrow" [reference to *Macbeth*] –is this our style of talk . . . What say you to the Regicide Empire of to-day? Tell me, my friend, do its terrors appal you into an abject submission, or rouse you to a vigorous defence? But do–I no longer prevent it–do go on–look into futurity. Has this Empire nothing to alarm you when all struggle against it is over, when Mankind shall be silent before it, when all nations shall be disarmed, disheartened and truly divided by a treacherous peace? (326)

The [French] Royal Family perished, because it was royal. The Nobles perished, because they were noble. The Men, Women and Children, who had property, because they had property to be robbed of. The Priests were punished, after they had been robbed of their all, not for their vices, but for their virtues and their piety, which made them an honour to their sacred profession, and to that nature, of which we ought to be proud, since they belong to it. (336)

The October Politician [William Eden] is so full of charity and good nature, that he supposes, that these very robbers and murderers themselves are in a course of amelioration; on what ground I cannot conceive, except on the long practice of every crime, and by its complete success. He is an Origenist, and believes in the conversion of the Devil. All that runs in the place of blood in his veins, is nothing but the milk of human kindness. (337)

[Origen (c. 184-c. 253) was an influential Church Father. In a notable dispute with a bishop, Origen was accused of teaching that Satan would eventually receive salvation, but he did not in fact teach that.]

But still our Author [William Eden] considers the confession as a proof, that "truth is making its way into their bosoms." No! it is not making its way into their bosoms. It has forced its way into their mouths! The evil spirit, by which they are possessed, though essentially a liar, is forced, by the tortures of conscience, to confess the truth; to confess enough for their condemnation, but not for their amendment. (338)

What seemed to us to be the best system of liberty that a nation ever enjoyed, to them seems the yoke of an intolerable slavery. This speculative faction had long been at work. The French Revolution did not cause it: it only discovered it, increased it, and gave fresh vigour to its operations. (352)

It is to delude ourselves to consider the state of France, since their Revolution, as a state of Anarchy. It is something far worse. Anarchy it is, undoubtedly, if compared with Government pursuing the peace, order, morals, and prosperity of the People. But regarding only the power that has really guided, from the day of the Revolution to this time, it has been of all Governments the most absolute, despotic, and effective, that has hitherto appeared on earth. Never were the views and politics of any Government pursued with half the regularity, system and method, that a diligent observer must have contemplated with amazement and terror in theirs. Their state is not an Anarchy, but a series of short-lived Tyrannies. (356) I hear it said too, that they have lately declared in favour of property. This is exactly of the same sort with the former. What need had they to make this declaration, if they did not know, that by their doctrines and practices they had totally subverted all property? What Government of Europe, either in its origin or its continuance, has thought it necessary to declare itself in favour of property? (373)

They renew their old fraudulent declaration against confiscations, and then they expressly exclude all adherents to their ancient lawful Government from any benefit of it: that is to say, they promise, that they will secure all their brother plunderers in their share of the common plunder. The fear of being robbed by every new succession of robbers, who do not keep even the faith of that kind of society, absolutely required, that they should give security to the dividends of Spoil; else they could not exist a moment. But it was necessary, in giving security to robbers, that honest men should be deprived of all hope of restitution; and thus their interests were made utterly and eternally incompatible. So that it appears, that this boasted security of property is nothing more than a seal put upon its destruction: this ceasing of confiscation is to secure the confiscators against the innocent proprietors. (374-375)

But I trust that our Countrymen will not be softened to that kind of crimes and criminals; for if we should, our hearts will be hardened to every thing which has a claim on our benevolence. A kind Providence has placed in our breasts a hatred of the unjust and cruel, in order that we may preserve ourselves from cruelty and injustice. They who bear cruelty, are accomplices in it. The pretended gentleness which excludes that charitable rancour, produces an indifference which is half an approbation. They never will love where they ought to love, who do not hate where they ought to hate. (375-376)

Enmity to us and to all civilized nations is wrought into the very stamina of its constitution [the current French rule]. It was made to pursue the purposes of that fundamental enmity. The design will go on regularly in every position and in every relation. Their hostility is to break us to their dominion: their amity is to debauch us to their principles. In the former we are to contend with their force; in the latter with their intrigues. But we stand in a very different posture of defence in the two situations. In war, so long as Government is supported, we fight with the whole united force of the kingdom. When under the name of peace the war of intrigue begins, we do not contend against our enemies with the whole force of the kingdom. (376-377)

The Jacobins [of England] are worse than lost to their country. Their hearts are abroad. Their sympathy with the Regicides of France is complete. Just as in a civil contest, they exult in all their victories; they are dejected and mortified in all their defeats. Nothing that the Regicides can do, (and they have laboured hard for the purpose) can alienate them from their cause. (378)

But, before this time, our liberty has never been corrupted. I mean to say, that it has never been debauched from its domestick relations. To this time it has been English Liberty, and English Liberty only. Our love of Liberty, and our love of our Country, were not distinct things. (383)

We are men, and as men, undoubtedly, nothing human is foreign to us. We cannot be too liberal in our general wishes for the happiness of our kind. But in all questions on the mode of procuring it for any particular community, we ought to be fearful of admitting those, who have no interest in it, or who have, perhaps, an interest against it, into the consultation. Above all, we cannot be too cautious in our communication with those, who seek their happiness by other roads than those of humanity, morals and religion, and whose liberty consists, and consists alone, in being free from those restraints, which are imposed by the virtues upon the passions. (383-384)

When we invite danger [such as radical politics] from a confidence in defensive measures, we ought, first of all, to be sure, that it is a species of danger against which any defensive measures, that can be adopted, will be sufficient. Next, we ought to know that the spirit of our Laws, or that our own dispositions, which are stronger than Laws, are susceptible of all those defensive measures which the occasion may require. A third consideration is whether these measures will not bring more odium than strength to Government; and the last, whether the authority that makes them, in a general corruption of manners and principles, can ensure their execution? Let no one argue from the state of things, as he sees them at present, concerning what will be the means and capacities of Government when the time arrives, which shall call for remedies commensurate to enormous evils.

It is an obvious truth, that no constitution can defend itself. It must be defended by the wisdom and fortitude of men. These are what no constitution can give. They are the gifts of God; and he alone knows, whether we shall possess such gifts at the time we stand in need of them. Constitutions furnish the civil means of getting at the natural; it is all that in this case they can do. But our Constitution has more impediments, than helps. Its excellencies, when they come to be put to this sort of proof, may be found among its defects. (384)

Such is the work. But miserable works have been defended by the constancy of the garrison. Weather-beaten ships have been brought safe to port by the spirit and alertness of the crew. (385)

But when these men themselves are the magistrates; when all the consequence, weight and authority of a great nation adopt them; when we see them conjoined with victory, glory, power and dominion, and homage paid to them by every Government, it is not possible that the downhill should not be slid into, recommended by every thing which has opposed it. Let it be remembered that no young man can go to any part of Europe without taking this place of pestilential contagion in his way: and whilst the less active part of the community will be debauched by this travel, whilst children are poisoned at these schools, our trade will put the finishing hand to our ruin. No factory will be settled in France, that will not become a club of complete French Jacobins. The minds of young men of that description will receive a taint in their religion, their morals, and their politicks, which they will in a short time communicate to the whole kingdom. (389)

[Burke is imagining a Jacobin future in England:]

Nobody will dare to censure that popular part of the tribunal, whose only restraint on misjudgment is the censure of the publick. They, who find fault with the decision, will be represented as enemies to the institution. Juries, that convict for the crown, will be loaded with obloquy. The Juries, who acquit, will be held up as models of justice. If Parliament orders a prosecution and fails, (as fail it will), it will be treated to its face as guilty of a conspiracy maliciously to prosecute. Its care in discovering a conspiracy against the state will be treated as a forged plot to destroy the liberty of the subject; every such discovery, instead of strengthening Government, will weaken its reputation. (392)

In a situation of fatal dependence on popularity, and without one aid from the little remaining power of the Crown, it is not to be expected that they will take on them that odium which more or less attaches upon every exertion of strong power. The Ministers of popularity will lose all their credit at a stroke, if they pursue any of those means necessary to give life, vigour, and consistence to Government. (393)

About the editors

Daniel Klein is professor of economics and JIN Chair at the Mercatus Center at George Mason University, where he and Erik Matson lead a program in Adam Smith. He is also research fellow at the Ratio Institute (Stockholm) and chief editor of *Econ Journal Watch*.

Dominic Pino holds an M.A. in economics from George Mason University and is a William F. Buckley Jr. Fellow in Political Journalism at National Review Institute.

CL Press
A Fraser Institute Project
https://clpress.net/

Professor Daniel Klein (George Mason University, Economics and Mercatus Center) and Dr. Erik Matson (Mercatus Center), directors of the Adam Smith Program at George Mason University, are the editors and directors of CL Press. CL stands at once for classical liberal and conservative liberal.

CL Press is a project of the Fraser Institute (Vancouver, Canada).

People:

Dan Klein and Erik Matson are the co-editors and executives of the imprint.

Jane Shaw Stroup is Editorial Advisor, doing especially copy-editing and text preparation.

An Advisory Board:

Jordan Ballor, *Center for Religion, Culture, and Democracy*
Caroline Breashears, *St. Lawrence Univ.*
Donald Boudreaux, *George Mason Univ.*
Ross Emmett, *Arizona State Univ.*
Knud Haakonssen, *Univ. of St. Andrews*
Björn Hasselgren, *Timbro, Uppsala Univ.*
Karen Horn, *Univ. of Erfurt*
Jimena Hurtado, *Univ. de los Andes*
Nelson Lund, *George Mason Univ.*
Daniel Mahoney, *Assumption Univ.*
Deirdre N. McCloskey, *Univ. of Illinois–Chicago*

Thomas W. Merrill, *American Univ.*
James Otteson, *Univ. of Notre Dame*
Catherine R. Pakaluk, *Catholic Univ. of America*
Sandra Peart, *Univ. of Richmond*
Mario Rizzo, *New York Univ.*
Loren Rotner, *Univ. of Austin*
Marc Sidwell, *New Culture Forum*
Craig Smith, *Univ. of Glasgow*
Emily Skarbek, *Brown Univ.*
David Walsh, *Catholic Univ. of America*
Richard Whatmore, *Univ. of St. Andrews*
Barry Weingast, *Stanford Univ.*
Lawrence H. White, *George Mason Univ.*
Amy Willis, *Liberty Fund*
Bart Wilson, *Chapman Univ.*
Todd Zywicki, *George Mason Univ.*

Why start CL Press?

CL Press publishes good, low-priced work in intellectual history, political theory, political economy, and moral philosophy. More specifically, CL Press explores and advance discourse in the following areas:

- The intellectual history and meaning of liberalism.

- The relationship between liberalism and conservatism.

- The role of religion in disseminating liberal understandings and institutions including: humankind's ethical universalism, the moral equality of souls, the rule of law, religious liberty, the meaning and virtues of economic life.

- The relationship between religion and economic philosophy.

- The political, social, and economic philosophy of the Scottish Enlightenment, especially Adam Smith.